GOD SPEAKS
AND
YOU CAN
Hear Him

Understaning Prophets, your Gift of Prophecy, and Keys to Cultivating a Healthy Prophetic Culture

EDGAR A. IRAHETA

God Speaks and You Can Hear Him

Copyright © 2017 by Edgar A. Iraheta.

Edgar A. Iraheta | permission@edgarandvictoria.org
177 Apostles Way, Box A, Santa Rosa Beach, Fl 32450.
http://www.edgarandvictoria.org

Cover Design by Pixelstudios at Fiverr.com

PRINT ISBN: 978-0-9991302-1-6

For eBook version visit: books.pronoun.com/edgariraheta/

First Edition: June 2017

10 9 8 7 6 5 4 3 2 1

Contents

FOREWORD

BY DR. BILL HAMON

Prophet Edgar has published the revelation for activation and maturing Christians in prophetic ministry. I have personally taught and mentored Edgar. He has traveled with me in ministry and helped me prophesy over many ministers and saints. Edgar has a proven ministry of a prophet.

The Lord spoke a prophecy to me through a major prophet in 1984, that I would have the "anointing and ministry of reproducing reproducers who would reproduce reproducers". Since that time there has been over 250,000 saints activated in the prophetic ministry and most of those have become reproducers of reproducers on every continent of the world. Edgar is one of those who has received the reproducing anointing.

He has a thorough Biblical knowledge with the ability to teach and impart what he ministers. Edgar's preaching and prophesying is with a powerful anointing.

Edgar also works with our prophetic evangelism teams who goes out weekly and prophesies and ministers healing and salvation to people out in the public marketplace.

Edgar has the ability to teach and train saints in the Spanish and English language. He is being mentored and matured to be one of the Christian International major ministers in the prophetic and apostolic demonstrating the Kingdom of God.

God bless you Edgar as you allow God to make you all He wants you to be and do in His Kingdom for His Church. This is just the first work you will produce in helping God's saints and ministers co-labor with Jesus to build His Church and demons-trate His Kingdom.

Your Bishop,

Apostle Bill Hamon

Bishop: Christian International Ministries Network (CIMN),Christian International Apostolic Network (CIAN) CI Global Network (CIGN)

Author: Author of 12 major books such as *"Prophets and Personal Prophecy", "Day Of The Saints"* plus 10 other Major Books on the Prophetic and Apostolic

COMMENDATION

APOSTLES TOM AND JANE HAMON

Apostles & Pastors of Vision Church @Christian International

In his book, God Speaks and You Can Hear Him, Edgar Iraheta provides valuable insight, personal experience and encouragement for every Believer to activate his or her ability to hear the Voice of the Lord. His teaching is scripturally sound and his challenge to each one is to move past the things that would act as road blocks of the anointing in our lives. We have personally watched Edgar grow and develop in his own gifts and ministry and are confident that this book will touch your heart, activate your spirit man and challenge you to a new place of intimacy with the Father.

As you read this book, allow the Holy Spirit to unlock and release the heart of God, the power of His Voice and the confidence of ministering His life to others through you.

Apostles Tom & Jane Hamon

A SPECIAL THANK YOU

I want to give honor and glory to Jesus Christ my King. In my darkest hour, He rescued me, called me, healed me, restored me, and gave me identity and purpose; I am yours forever.

I want to thank God for my parents, Jorge and Deysi Iraheta. I am here today because of your love, faith, support, and above all, your prayers and sacrifices. Thank you for believing in God's call in my life, for supporting me and for teaching me the importance of perseverance and diligence in responding to this call. Love you very much. I honor and thank you for bringing me into this world.

Also, I want to thank my pastors and spiritual parents, Apostle Tom and Jane Hamon, who always encouraged me to live the purpose and call of God for my life. They instilled in me the conviction that great things are always about to happen, and because of this, I have seen the goodness of God manifested in my life.

Your prophetic words and impartation in my life have launched me into my destiny in God. My heart is full of gratitude.

I would like to also honor Bishop Hamon and Mom "Evelyn" Hamon, who from the time I met them, I felt the love of God pouring into my heart.

Lastly, my beautiful wife, Victoria and our two handsome sons, Josiah and David. Words can only express a small drop of my love for you!

INTRODUCTION

Everyone has their favorite preacher, author, or motivational speaker. We value and appreciate what they have to say because we have found, if you will, our voice in them. They can give sound to our deepest desires. They empower our craziest dreams and ideas. We believe they believe in us. They have tapped into a part of our design by God that was meant to hear words that give purpose, direction, and power.

You and I have the greatest preacher, motivational speaker and coach in life. As a matter of fact, you have a team that is rooting for you, believing in you and ready to speak, willing to listen and strategize to help you reach your greatest potential. Our team is composed of God the Father, Son and Holy Spirit. The Father and Son decided to let the Holy Spirit be the team leader that would speak on their behalf. So, every time you need help, direction or even encouragement, you have access to a top-notch team (John 16:13).

Our relationship with the Holy Spirit is the most important one we can have today. Through Him, we are guided and led into all truth; we can hear words that affirm, confirm and empower God's plan for our life. It is through His Holy Spirit that we can hear the Voice of God and know the will of the Father; we can grasp the plans and designs of Heaven for our life, ministry or business. Jesus said that it would be the Holy Spirit's job to "declare" all things about Jesus and the Father (John 16: 8-15).

For this reason, Jesus Himself promised "And I will ask the Father, and he will give you another Helper, to be with you forever, even the Spirit of truth, whom the world cannot receive, because it neither sees him nor knows him. You know him, for he dwells with you and will be in you. "I will not leave you as orphans; I will come to you." (John 14:16–18, ESV)

Hearing the Voice of God is found in the depths, yet most simple whisper we experience from God daily. God, the Father, has and will always speak to us in several ways and at different times. His voice and heart had never been louder than when it was revealed by His Son, Jesus (Hebrews 1:1-4).

My hope and prayer are that you will be able to discover how God speaks to you. That you will learn how to develop your spiritual gift, how to prophesy, how to reach the lost and more than anything that you've encountered—God. That you will draw closer to Him, that you will have an undeniable touch from Him that will change you forever.

CHAPTER 1

The Prophetic Movement

The Prophetic Movement has been designed by the Holy Spirit to bring full recognition, restoration and activation of prophets and the prophetic ministry. The Church desperately needs a greater understanding of the office of prophet. It needs to know the prophet's anointing, authority, calling, ministry and purpose; how the prophet relates to the other fivefold ministers; and how we can properly respond with a right attitude toward God's prophets.

Dr. Bill Hamon
"Prophets and the Prophetic Movement: God's Prophetic Move Today"

The Book of Acts reveals the Supernatural model of the Church that Christ demonstrated for us to establish His Kingdom here on earth. We see that the Church went through a lot of persecution; however, it grew more and more. Supernatural events abounded: the blind received sight, those tormented by demons were delivered, the sick were healed, and the dead were raised and so on. We clearly see the Fivefold Ministry, equipping all the saints through supernatural impartation, following the doctrine (teachings) of Jesus Christ through the Apostles. We see the

11

Apostles, Prophets, Evangelists, Pastors, and Teachers fully functioning.

The Supernatural Church was birthed on the Day of Pentecost. It was a supernatural spiritual Body of Citizens of Heaven, advancing the Kingdom of God.

We are now in a time of restoration, where the Spirit of God is moving in His Church as in the days of its birth. Holy Spirit has been commissioned to restore, reform, and empower the Bride of Christ. Part of that restoration, has been the revelation of the proper function of the Fivefold Ministry and exercise of the Gifts of the Holy Spirit. Yet, millions of believers have not yet received the revelation of the gifts of the Holy Spirit and the Fivefold Ministry. We should, therefore, bring this revelation to the Body of Christ as members.

THE DECLINE OF
THE SUPERNATURAL CHURCH

In 312, before engaging Maxentius in battle, the Roman emperor Constantine prayed to the 'Supreme God' for help. Then he was given a sign, a cross in the noonday sky 'above the sun' with the words, 'Conquer by this.' That night, Constantine had a dream in which Christ told him to use the 'Chi-Rho' sign, the first two letters of Christ's name in Greek, 'as a safeguard in all engagements with his enemies.' The historian Lactantius records that Constantine ordered that this 'Chi-Rho' sign be written on the shields of all his soldiers. Constantine then defeated Maxentius as he marched on Rome. At the traditional place of this encounter an inscription reads: 'In this sign you will conquer. Good Christian, do not pass the spot without recognizing Jesus Christ our Redeemer. Praise be to Jesus Christ forever and ever. Amen.'

-Mark Water (The Christian Book of Records)

From this vision a decree was issued that began the fall of the Supernatural Church. You may ask why? The decree gave Christianity along with other religions, the freedom of religious expression. Christians felt relief from the persecution that plagued their daily life. Providing for them an opportunity of freedom, to grow and expand. This all sound like benefits, rather then things that would cause a great falling away.

The Church thrives and grows best when it's in direct opposition to the Kingdom of Darkness. With the increased freedom, no one would dare speak against Christians or any religion, as there was freedom of expression. But there are dangers, as the Church can become apathetic and lethargic. Even in freedom, we were designed to thrive, but only by staying in direct conflict with the works of the enemy.

It was seventy years later that Emperor Theodosius made it mandatory for every person to convert to Christianity. As a result, the Church lost the power of the Cross, the Blood of Jesus and Repentance. Salvation no longer was about a supernatural transformation of the heart. This edict demanded that every Roman citizen converts to Christianity to occupy a position in politics, business and be a citizen of Rome.

> Theodosius not only demanded adherence to Christianity, but he undertook the forcible suppression of all other religions and prohibited idol worship. Under his decrees, heathen temples were torn down and there was much bloodshed among the heathen priests and worshipers. (What a reversal from less than a century before!) The military spirit of Imperial Rome had entered the Church. Christianity appeared to have conquered the whole Empire, but by making the Church over into its own image, the Roman Empire had conquered the Spiritual Church.

Dr. Bill Hamon (The Eternal Church: A Prophetic Look at the
Church-Her History, Restoration, and Destiny.)

The Church changed from supernatural and turned into
a political and structured organization. During this time,
many true Christians were political officials, businessmen,
etc. Ironically, it seemed like a great blessing to the spread
of Christianity, but it was the enemy's strategy to bring
the Church a thousand years of darkness and deterioration
(Middle Ages).

For a thousand years, the Supernatural Spiritual Church
which was birthed at Pentecost went into a state of apostasy.
Many of these present truths were lost. In 1500, God in His
sovereignty began to restore the Church by the Reformers,
Martin Luther being the first.

RESTORATION OF ALL THINGS: A PROPHETIC DECREE.

God was not surprised by the thousand years of darkness
which the Church lived. He always has a perfect plan. In
the Book of Acts, we see a prophetic promise made to us
which we are still living. This promise is restoration. If you
read what the Apostles and the early Church did, it is an
example of what we are to live and overcome. We are living
in the most powerful times in the history of the Church.
The perfect plan of God is preparing His Bride and Jesus
Christ paid the price with His own Body and Blood.

He gave us gifts and ministries so that we will establish
His Ekklesia and Kingdom here on earth:

A restoration movement is when God brings revelation by the Holy
Spirit to men and women of God on some truths that you want to

revive in the Church. The "times of restoration" prophesied in Acts 3:21 beginning in 1500. A.D. continues to the present time. There have been five restoration movements since that date; only two or three must still take place to fulfill the prophecy of the Apostle Peter in Acts 3:18-25 (The Day of the Saints - by Dr. Bill Hamon)

Acts 3:20-21 says,

"that He may send Jesus Christ, who was preached to you before, 21 whom heaven must receive until the times of restoration of all things, which God has spoken by the mouth of all His holy prophets since the world began."

The word of God reveals to us that it is necessary that heaven receives Jesus Christ until the *"times of restoration of all things"* is fulfilled. The Heavens are holding back Jesus Christ because this decree has not been fulfilled. When the times of restoration is fulfilled, Jesus will come to find a perfect, complete, pure Bride and ready to rule and reign with Him.

In the last 500 years, there has been a powerful restoration movement. The doctrines of Jesus Christ were lost in the time of the great fall of the Church, and the Fivefold Ministry stopped functioning, but now we see its restoration. We are now in a time of Reformation.

In 2008, Jesus began the Third and Final Apostolic Reformation of His Church; this was decreed and declared by Bishop Bill Hamon. This was then confirmed by many prophets in the last seven years. This Final Reformation, will bring the perfection of the Ekklesia that is can be mobilized to transform the Kingdoms of the World into the Kingdoms of our Lord and Christ. Now, let's see what has been restored in the last 500 years:

WHAT HAS BEEN RESTORED IN THE LAST 500 YEARS

Year	Movements of Resto-ration	Truth Restored
1500	The Protestant Move-ment	Salvation by grace through faith (Eph. 2:8-9).
1600	The Puritan Movement	Water baptism, separation of church and state.
1700	The Holiness Move-ment	Holiness, the Church becomes separated from the world.
1800	The Movement of Di-vine Holiness	Divine holiness for the body.
1900	The Pentecostal Move-ment	The baptism of the Holy Spirit and speaking in tongues
1950	The Movement of the Latter Rain	Prophetic Presbytery, praise, and worship.
1970	The Movement of Pros-perity	Faith declarations, pros-perity.
1980	The Prophetic Move-ment	The Prophets and the Gifts of the Holy Spirit
1990	The Apostolic Move-ment	The Apostles
By Dr. Bill Hamon, "The Prophets and Prophetic Move-ment" Pg. 34 and 35		
USED WITH PERMISSION		

WHY IS THE PROPHETIC MOVEMENT IMPORTANT?

First, we must know that every move of restoration is a door for another move of God. The Prophetic Movement was birthed, to pave the way for the restoration of the Apostolic Movement. The Apostle was the last of the five ascension gifts that were restored. Now, this Apostolic Movement has brought the Movement of the Saints.

In every movement, the Holy Spirit has restored truths and spiritual experiences that Jesus revealed. When something is restored in the Church, a part of her identity is renewed or restored to its original state. Jesus Christ was the perfect minister and example for us. He fulfilled the mandate of the Fivefold Ministry. He was the Great Apostle, Prophet, Teacher, Evangelist, and Pastor (Ephesians 4:11). Each gift was commissioned for the purpose of building an empowered Church.

What is important about the Prophetic Movement? It's that it has restored to the Church the ministry of the Prophet, which Jesus demonstrated and established to equip the saints for the work of prophetic ministry. If this revelation is not understood or received, it can bring destruction to the Church. Prophets exist today, and many believers do not receive the Prophets of God because there is a lack of true understanding of the Prophet and the prophetic gifts.

> "Participants in the Prophetic Movement need to be aware that the movement itself is not the goal, but rather the means to the ultimate goal." -Bishop Bill Hamon, "The Prophets and Prophetic Movement."

WHAT DID THE PROPHETIC MOVEMENT RESTORE?

The Prophetic Movement restored and gave due recognition to the office of the Prophet. When you honor and receive the Prophet, God's Word says that one receives the prophet's reward. Today, thousands of believers have been trained in their prophetic gift. Before this move of restoration there was a shortage of the prophetic ministry. Now there are many ministries and training conferences to equip the saints in their gifts.

PRIMARY THINGS RESTORED IN THE PROPHETIC MOVEMENT:

- **The Prophets** – A Prophet's role in equipping, maturing and exercising their gift of ascension has been restored.
- **Prophetic Ministers** - Prophetic Saints, Prophetic People (Different Terms can be used to describe people who believe and move under a prophetic anointing) — a saint does not need to have one of the gifts of Christ's ascension to be a prophetic minister. A prophetic minister flows in the supernatural gifts of the Holy Spirit. A prophetic people acknowledge that the apostles and prophets have been restored and move under the apostolic and prophetic grace.
- **Personal prophecy** — before, it was rare to hear personal prophecy, yet there was also little heard that someone would prophesy in the congregation. Now, we see that this has been restored. Before, it was the work of a few Prophets who would minister, but now, a prophetic people have been raised, which prophesy and minister God's Voice.
- **The Prophetic Presbytery** — are ministers of the Word of God to His people. Prophets who have been tested in their ministry for years. Their function is to

ordain a Minister in his call for any specific need or to any person.

- **The Gifts of the Holy Spirit** — all authentic movements of restoration bring revelation and divine wisdom to enable the people in their spiritual gifts. The Prophetic Movement is to activate the prophetic gift and the gifts of the Holy Spirit to His people.

The Prophetic Movement is to proclaim God's prophets, to spread the prophetic, and enable others to become prophetic ministers and produce a prophetic people for the purpose of God. - Bishop Bill Hamon

---

WHY IS IT IMPORTANT TO HAVE A MENTALITY OF RESTORATION?

The believer who does not have a mentality of restoration will miss the next move of God. We are in times of reformation, revival and spiritual awakening. God is not only the God of yesterday; He is the God of yesterday, today, tomorrow, and forever. Whenever God causes a new movement in the body, those who have not renewed their minds are those who criticize the movement and get stuck. We cannot have a fear of the extremes; it is better to be passionate and excited than to be apathetic and stagnant in the revelation of yesterday.

As leaders, its wise to examine where our Churches are in God's timeline of restoration. As saints its important that we encourage the Body of Christ to continue in step with everything in Gods agenda. You're called to be an agent of restoration, accept your calling and commission.

CHAPTER 2

GOD STILL SPEAKS TODAY!

"My sheep hear My voice, and I know them, and they follow Me."

(John 10:27)

Our God is a personal God. He desires intimate fellowship with individuals more than a distant relationship with humanity as a race. When Adam and Eve were the entire race, the Almighty walked and talked with them. But ever since sin dulled human ears to hearing and human eyes to seeing God, He has not been able to communicate with everyone individually. The race as a whole does not desire His fellowship and is not sensitive enough to hear His voice.

Dr. Bill Hamon

Prophets & Personal Prophecy

In early 2001, I began a season of searching for God, I was 16 years old, but had a profound desire to encounter God and serve Him. I did everything I knew to grasp some sense of peace, understanding, and knowledge of Him. I've always been an avid reader, but no matter what book I read, I felt as if God was nowhere to be found. I learned many valuable disciplines, truths, and principles about the Kingdom of God, but it felt as if God Himself was far from me. I watched every preacher on every Christian Network asking God to touch my life like those on TV. I fasted, prayed, read my Bible and felt the most unfulfilled ever. By around late 2002, I had resigned myself to simply living the nominal Christian life. Attend Church, its functions and stay out of trouble.

This profound hunger was birthed in part out of the pain of my past. I had a lot of unresolved issues from past abuse in my childhood, and I needed God to erase my past and bring peace to me from all I had lived growing up. I grew up silently carrying the pain and hurt. My prayer life was what I would call filled with anguish and hunger; anguish because I had a sense that no matter what I tried, I could not reach God; hunger because all I could do was long to know He was there.

In the summer of 2003, I went through three months of intense prayer; I had drawn, if you will, the line in the sand. I had given God an ultimatum. For three months, I pointed the finger at God, every night with tears in my eyes I would cry out to Him and tell Him, that I wanted to know He heard me and that I wanted to serve Him with everything in me.

Suddenly, I find myself at a seminar where they teach people how to hear the voice of God. They were teaching a class called "Ministering Spiritual Gifts." A company of prophets had come from the Panhandle of Florida to do this training; they said they were from Christian International and that Dr. Bill Hamon was the father of the prophetic movement. So I took a lot of interest, and I needed to be there, although with a lot of hesitation. The event was hosted at a Presbyterian Church, which made it even more interesting. These guys say they hear from God, that there is a father of the prophetic movement and that they can teach me how to hear from God! I'll be honest with you; I don't remember anything they taught because I was not there to learn, I was there to hear God speak to me.

It was at that time that I found myself seated in a chair, and a Prophet named Jimmy Kellet was making his way down the line, prophesying to people. I remember watching intently, thinking to myself, why are they crying? Why are they so touched by what he was saying? It was then my turn, he asked for my name and began to pray, and then he said:

> Brother, God has really shown me that there are some areas that you've been very pointed with God about it, and it's like you have taken an arrow, and you just keep poking God, "Come on God, have you heard my prayers; I've got to hear what's going on here. And God says: "Son, know that I'm releasing my anointing so that you can hear what I'm saying. But He said: "But son, I've also answered your prayers. Yes and Amen. So son, quit pushing on them and just take the peace and He says as peace comes, you are going to see the fulfillment of your dreams.

Even as I remember that day, I can't help but have tears of joy in my eyes. My Heavenly Father had heard my prayers, and I knew at that moment without any question that I would never again doubt if He could speak to me. He knew intimately every detail of my life, and He had a plan for my life. Ever since that moment, a passion for helping others hear God's voice was birthed. I moved to Christian International Ministries Network September 2005 to begin my training at their Vision Leadership Institute (Formerly known as Ministry Training College).

I became a son of the House of the Prophets and now live every day with a passion for demonstrating that God speaks and you can hear him.

I share this testimony with you, because you may find yourself in the same place at this very moment. Don't quit, don't stop crying out. Don't give up, He will speak to you, and as you discover the keys to hearing Him, you will become an instrument in His hands of purpose and destiny. You will unlock the future of other sons and daughters.

In this chapter, I want to help you recognize that God still speaks today; and learn what the three major hindrances to hearing the voice of God are.

WE WILL ANSWER THESE COMMON QUESTIONS

Does God still speak to us today?
If He does, why does He want to communicate with us?
Is it common for Him to speak and communicate with us?

HE WANTS TO SPEAK TO YOU!

Psalm 139:1-6 says,

> "O Lord, you have searched me and known me! You know when I sit down and when I rise up; you discern my thoughts from a far. You search out my path and my lying down and are acquainted with

all my ways. Even before a word is on my tongue, behold, O Lord, you know it altogether. You hem me in, behind and before, and lay your hand upon me. Such knowledge is too wonderful for me; it is high; I cannot attain it."

King David was a man who had an intimate relationship with God. Here, he describes how he feels about God and His Presence. He realizes God knows everything about him; he knew this because God spoke to him later (Verse 17 & 18), he says "How precious to me are your thoughts, O God! How vast is the sum of them! If I would count them, they are more than the sand. I awake, and I am still with you."

God's heart and desire are to speak to us because He wants to share how He feels about us, to reveal our destiny and purpose, to guide us and direct us. He wants us to know, that He is a relational God. Not a distant, far-off, non-relational God. He is the God, who searches our hearts, knows our thoughts, knows our words, and knows our purpose, calling and destiny. From the very beginning of time, His plan was to walk with us, speak with us, and relate to us.

OUR HEART DESIRES TO HEAR HIM!

"My heart has heard you say, "Come and talk with me." And my heart responds, "Lord, I am coming." (Psalm 27:8, NLT)

Often, I hear people say, *I want to have a better relationship with God!* One scripture that changed my life forever was Psalm 27:8. We often don't realize that the longings and desires of our heart, like *"I want to know you God!"* is our spirit man responding to the call of God.

We must recognize and discern these promptings. He calls us and our heart answers. In those times, we can begin to experience His presence, voice, and power in a new way, falling in love with Him! Drawing closer and learning to hear Him and be led by Him. Often, we ignore these promptings because of the busyness of life and cares of the world.

Two years before receiving that prophetic word that forever changed my life, I was being prompted by God to come to Him. My hunger, even though it was pain at times from my past, was God's gentle whisper saying, come this way, I am ready to heal and restore. Sometimes, we may ask ourselves, why didn't God just say something at that moment? We may get a sense that maybe God is wasting our time, but there is no wasted time in any of God's perfect processes for our life. During those years, I learned to seek Him in ways that I to this day still use. Disciplines of searching His word for revelation and understanding, prayer and fasting to stay close to Him and keep my spirit man in tune.

Whatever you have been practicing, if it's a Kingdom Principle, it's not a wasted time, you will reap the reward of your diligence and faithfulness to Him.

GOD HAS ALWAYS SPOKEN!

- Adam and Eve in Genesis 2:16, 3:8-17.
- Abraham in Genesis 21:1-7, 13:14; 15:1-9; 17:9-22; 18:1-20; 20:3-7; 21:12-17; 22:1-15.
- Moses in Exodus 3:14, etc.
- Joshua in Joshua 5:14, 15, etc.
- King David in 1 Samuel 23.

Do you believe God wants to speak to you today? If He spoke to Adam and Eve, Abraham, Moses and Joshua, King David, don't you think He wants to speak to us today?

> "Long ago God spoke in many different ways to our fathers through the prophets, in visions, dreams, and even face-to-face, telling them little by little about his plans. But now in these days he has spoken to us through his Son to whom he has given everything and through whom he made the world and everything there is." (Hebrews 1:1–2; TLB)

I know, you may say, but this was in the Old Testament. Let's look at the New Testament.

NEW TESTAMENT

Jesus said, *"My sheep hear my voice, and I know them, and they follow me"* (John 10:27; ESV). And most would argue, He said that to His disciples, but a little later He says *"And I have other sheep that are not of this fold. I must bring them also, and they will listen to my voice. So there will be one flock, one shepherd"* (John 10:16, ESV). God's leading and voice through His Son are still active today, and He speaks through His Holy Spirit.

Paul - Acts 9:3, 4, 27:23, 24.
Peter - Acts 10:3, 13.
John - The Book of Revelation
Hebrews 1:1 declares:

> "Long ago, at many times and in many ways, God spoke to our fathers by the prophets,"

GOD SPEAKS

I alluded earlier to the value of learning the ways that God speaks to us today—the disciplines and principles of His Kingdom. Like His Written Word, but at the same time, He speaks to us through His:

Prophets & Personal Prophecy

Sons and Daughters

And again, the Ministry of Jesus is still active today, through His Holy Spirit. But also, we must see all Scriptural experiences as an example of how God can speak to us. For example, we find in scripture that God used:

Angels to speak

Dreams and Visions

God is still speaking today!

GOD'S VOICE

Hearing the Voice of God brings a manifestation of God's Kingdom in our life.

Intimacy- When God speaks, His desire is to draw us closer to Him, to guide us and direct us. This only happens through an intimate relationship. Friends share thoughts, ideas, and dreams. Jesus said *"I no longer call you slaves, because a master doesn't confide in his slaves. Now you are my friends, since I have told you everything the Father told me."* (John 15:15; NLT)

Revelation and Wisdom - *"Call to me and I will answer you, and will tell you great and hidden things that you have not known."* (Jeremiah 33:3; ESV)

Deliverance & Protection - *"When he calls to me, I will answer him; I will be with him in trouble; I will rescue him and honor him."* (Psalm 91:15; ESV)

Blessings- When we obey the voice of God, we will see blessings upon our lives. *""And if you faithfully obey the voice of the Lord your God, being careful to do all his commandments that I command you today, the Lord your God will set you high above all the nations of the earth. And all these blessings shall come upon you and overtake you, if you obey the voice of the Lord your God."* (Deuteronomy 28:1–2; ESV)

And much more!

WHAT HINDERS US FROM HEARING HIS VOICE?

"My people are destroyed for lack of knowledge; because you have rejected knowledge, I reject you from being a priest to me. And since you have forgotten the law of your God, I also will forget your children." (Hosea 4:6; ESV)

"Oh come, let us worship and bow down; let us kneel before the Lord, our Maker! For he is our God, and we are the people of his pasture, and the sheep of his hand. Today, if you hear his voice, do not harden your hearts, as at Meribah, as on the day at Massah in the wilderness, when your fathers put me to the test and put me to the proof, though they had seen my work. For forty years I loathed that generation and said, "They are a people who go astray in their heart, and they have not known my ways." Therefore I swore in my wrath, "They shall not enter my rest."" (Psalm 95:6–11; ESV)

The biggest hindrance to hearing the voice of God is Lack of Knowledge, also known as ignorance. This produces a life of limitations, uncertainty, and frustration. In my journey in seeking God, I discovered truths about God that I had never experienced in my life. Truths, like God, speaks today; He can heal and deliver you from sickness and demonic oppression.

1 Corinthians 12:1: *"Now concerning spiritual gifts, brethren, I do not want you to be ignorant."* The Apostle Paul knew the importance of the Corinthian Church being knowledgeable in the spiritual gifts that God had for them, in the same way, we cannot remain ignorant and must begin to learn, exercise and demonstrate the God we read of in Scripture.

Are you ready to learn to hear His Voice in your life and to be a voice of God for others?

ACTIVATION

"Activations" are opportunities for you to stir up the gifts of God inside of you.

2 Timothy 1:6–7 (ESV) — *For this reason I remind you to fan into flame the gift of God, which is in you through the laying on of my hands, for God gave us a spirit not of fear but of power and love and self-control.*

Through stirring or fanning into flame the gifts of God, we can exercise our senses to discern the voice of God.

Hebrews 5:14 (ESV) — *But solid food is for the mature, for those who have their powers of discernment trained by constant practice to distinguish good from evil.*

Activation | *Writing the Thoughts of God*

Description | In this activation, we are going to ask God to speak to us by writing down His thoughts.

The Lord says...._____

_____

_____

_____

_____

_____

_____

_____

_____

_____

_____

_____

_____

_____

_____

_____

_____

_____

_____

_____

_____

_____

_____

_____

_____

_____

_____

_____

_____

_____

_____

_____

CHAPTER 3

TRAINING TO HEAR

"But solid food is for the mature, for those who have their powers of discernment trained by constant practice to distinguish good from evil."

(Hebrews 5:14, ESV)

Teaching vs. Activating. We are not jaust talking about teaching the saints. Present-truth believers have been taught about the gifts of the Spirit for the last eighty years. Teaching alone does not fulfill the minister's responsibility anymore. All present-truth ministers must now motivate, activate and mature the saints in their gifts and calling.

Dr. Bill Hamon

Prophets and the Prophetic Movement

Hebrews 1:1-2 it says that *"Long ago, at many times and in many ways, God spoke to our fathers by the prophets, but in these last days he has spoken to us by his Son, whom he appointed the heir of all things, through whom also he created the world."*

We find throughout all scripture that God has been faithful to reveal Himself to man and woman who were ready to hear Him and obey His voice. When people refused to hear Him, or obey, time and time again, He would go to great lengths to find a way to reach them. Ultimately, He sent His Son to speak to us, The Word becoming Flesh that we may hear directly from Him and have access to Him (John 1).

You may ask yourself, but

How do I discern His voice?

How do I fine-tune my spiritual ears to hear Him?

Is there a specific way He speaks to me?

How do I develop my spiritual gift?

Let's take a closer look at a specific passage of the Scripture that will shed some light into how we can learn to discern or distinguish His voice.

> "But solid food belongs to those who are of full age, that is, those who by reason of use have their senses exercised to discern both good and evil." (Hebrews 5:14; NKJV)

Let's read this in some other translations:

> "But solid food is for the mature, who because of practice have their senses trained to discern good and evil." (NASB95)

"Solid food is for those who are mature, who through training have the skill to recognize the difference between right and wrong." (NLT)

There are two important things we can learn from this scripture:

- In order to develop in maturity and discernment (our ability to distinguish or hear the voice of God), we have to exercise, practice and train our senses to tell the difference between what is right and wrong, good and evil.
- It lets us know that it is not for a few special gifted people; it is for those who are willing to train, to get equipped, and learn to exercise their spiritual senses—those willing to develop their spiritual skills. We should stop thinking only a few "spiritual" people can hear from God.

Now, what is the context of this scripture? Let's back it up and read why the writer of Hebrews is saying this:

"There is much more we would like to say about this, but it is difficult to explain, especially since you are spiritually dull and don't seem to listen. You have been believers so long now that you ought to be teaching others. Instead, you need someone to teach you again the basic things about God's word. You are like babies who need milk and cannot eat solid food. For someone who lives on milk is still an infant and doesn't know how to do what is right." (Hebrews 5:11–13; NLT)

In other words, the context is, you should be teachers, you should be sharp, strong and skilled in discerning what God is saying, but instead, I must lay down the foundation, the elem-entary principles once again, I should retrain you, get you to exercise and practice again until you become mature.

We can conclude two things from this:

- We must train, practice and exercise to grow in anything.
- We must train, practice and exercise to maintain that level of skill and move on to greater levels.

There are two types of discernment; one is natural and the other is spiritual. The Word *"discern"* according to the Concise Oxford English Dictionary means *"recognize or find out, showing good judgment, to separate, distinguish between."*

Let's look at a practical natural application to explain this:

Natural discernment is developed through training

1. Our natural senses are trained to discern between two natural objects
   a. Practical illustration:
      ○ Example: Is it an apple or an orange?
        - **Sight:** it looks like an apple.
        - **Touch:** it feels like an apple.
        - **Hearing:** it sounds like an apple when it is sliced or bitten.
        - **Smell:** it smells like an apple.
          - **Taste:** it tastes like an apple.
          - **Discernment:** it is an apple, not an orange.

Through exercise, practice, and training, we can learn the difference between one thing and another. Or give an accurate judgment of a specific thing. It is important that we as saints, prophets and a prophetic people learn to discern correctly so we can bring Glory to God through our prophetic ministry.

HOW DO I FINE-TUNE MY HEART AND SPIRITUAL EARS TO HEAR HIM?

The Question that now comes up is what should we practice, what should we exercise and train in? To fine-tune your heart and ears to the Voice of God, there are three important keys that will help you:

PRACTICE HIS PRESENCE

"Where shall I go from your Spirit? Or where shall I flee from your presence? If I ascend to heaven, you are there! If I make my bed in Sheol, you are there! If I take the wings of the morning and dwell in the uttermost parts of the sea, even there your hand shall lead me, and your right hand shall hold me. If I say, "Surely the darkness shall cover me, and the light about me be night," even the darkness is not dark to you; the night is bright as the day, for darkness is as light with you. For you formed my inward parts; you knitted me together in my mother's womb. I praise you, for I am fearfully and wonderfully made. Wonderful are your works; my soul knows it very well." (Psalm 139:7–14; ESV)

King David had such an awareness of the presence of God that no matter what he tried to do to get away, he could not. Activating the Gifts of God in your life will not be hard; the most difficult thing will be for you to stay in His presence, where you can continually be filled with His love and presence.

Many know about God, but few know God. Only *"the people who know their God shall stand firm and take action."* (Daniel 11:32; ESV)

To practice His Presence, you must spend TIME! The more time we spend with the Holy Spirit, the more clearly, we will hear His voice!

"So Jesus said to them, "Truly, truly, I say to you, the Son can do nothing of his own accord, but only what he sees the Father doing. For whatever the Father does, that the Son does likewise. For the Father loves the Son and shows him all that he himself is doing. And greater works than these will he show him, so that you may marvel." (John 5:19–20; ESV)

""I still have many things to say to you, but you cannot bear them now. When the Spirit of truth comes, he will guide you into all the truth, for he will not speak on his own authority, but whatever he hears he will speak, and he will declare to you the things that are to come. He will glorify me, for he will take what is mine and declare it to you. All that the Father has is mine; therefore I said that he will take what is mine and declare it to you." (John 16:12–15; ESV)

Jesus ministry flowed out of the intimate relationship He had with the Father and Holy Spirit. Everything He did and said came from the Father. Having an intimate relationship with the Father through Jesus Christ is what gives us access to His plans, answers, direction, and purpose in life. Notice it says that *"The Father will show him how to do even greater works than..."* The Father is ready to teach us what to do through intimacy, prayer, and relationship.

TRAIN YOUR GIFT(S)

We must learn to stir up the gifts of God inside of us by "building yourselves up in your most holy faith and praying in the Holy Spirit...," (Jude 20)

1 Corinthians 14:4 *The one who speaks in a tongue builds up himself but the one who prophesies builds up the church.*

One of the most powerful gifts the Holy Spirit has given you is speaking in Tongues (1 Corinthians 12:1-11). Dr. Bill Hamon says it's your power generator. Through speaking in tongues, we stir the power of God in us; we stir the anointing, gifts, and callings He has deposited inside of us.

Many are yet to learn how to tap into this and therefore, lacks power and presence in their lives. The Holy Spirit is our guide and friend; He will teach us, and as we pray in Tongues, new rivers of revelation are unlocked.

> "For this reason I remind you to fan into flame the gift of God, which is in you through the laying on of my hands, for God gave us a spirit not of fear but of power and love and self-control." (2 Timothy 1:6–7; ESV)

Part of the training is to learn what the gifts are; in Chapter 5, we will look at what the *"Prophetic Gifts"* are. It has been said that for you to become an expert in a certain field, you need 10,000 hours of teaching, practice, and hands-on training. The Apostle Paul said, *"Now concerning spiritual gifts, brothers, I do not want you to be uninformed."* (1 Corinthians 12:1; ESV)

EXERCISE YOUR GIFT(S)

Every athlete must practice in order to build their skills that their sports require for them to win. In the same manner, we as believers must exercise and practice to develop and grow in our spiritual skills (gifts) that will prepare us to win and succeed. One of the ways that will give an opportunity to practice and exercise our spiritual gifts is through activations. Dr. Bill Hamon coined this word and method to help activate saint's spirituals gifts and provide for them a safe environment where they could learn and practice. Through activations, you will have plenty of chances to exercise your gifts. The best environment to exercise in is a safe one. That is why during activations, we give each other permission to practice and take the risk.

Take every opportunity offered to you, with friends, family, ministers to learn and exercise your gifts until you are strong. Don't wait for you to be perfect, you never will. **2 Corinthians 13:9 says** *"For we know in part and we prophesy in part,"* we are always growing, strengthening, maturing in our gifts.

ACTIVATION

"Activations" are opportunities for you to stir up the gift of God inside of you.

2 Timothy 1:6–7 (ESV) — *For this reason I remind you to fan into flame the gift of God, which is in you through the laying on of my hands, for God gave us a spirit not of fear but of power and love and self-control.*

Through stirring or fanning into flame the gifts of God, we can exercise our senses to discern the voice of God.

Hebrews 5:14 (ESV) — *But solid food is for the mature, for those who have their powers of discernment trained by constant practice to distinguish good from evil.*

Activation: Prayer for a Loved One

Description: In this activation, we are going to ask God to give to **us** a thought, word of encouragement or prayer for a loved one or friend.

Instructions: Pick a person you would like to pray for and ask God to speak to you about. It can be a close friend or family member. As we pray, begin to *see, hear and sense* anything God has for them. Write down what God spoke to you for them. Take some time share it with them. A simple way of doing this could be for you to simply call them and ask them how they are doing, then begin to say...I was praying for you and I had this thought....

Variation: Instead of praying in your natural language, this time, pray in the Spirit, go silent and hear, sense, feel; it may be a picture or a thought that God gives you. Share that thought with them.

As I was praying for you, I felt from God....

_____

_____

_____

_____

_____

_____

_____

_____

_____

_____

_____

_____

_____

_____

_____

_____

_____

_____

_____

_____

CHAPTER 4

WAYS GOD SPEAKS

"Long ago God spoke in many different ways to our fathers through the prophets, in visions, dreams, and even face-to-face, telling them little by little about his plans."

(Hebrews 1:1, TLB)

LISTEN! What do you hear? Nothing? Good. Now you are ready to hear the voice of God. You were created in the likeness and image of God, and this is in your blood, your bones, your heart, and your DNA. You may not always behave like God, certainly most of us don't think like Him, but we have the ability to hear God. Why would He create you for the sole purpose of friendship and relationship and then make it impossible for you to hear His voice? He is speaking, and because we don't recognize the simplicity of His mannerism and His appearance, we ignore it.

Prophet Kim Clement

Call Me Crazy, But I'm Hearing God

I n the last chapter, we saw the importance of training, practice, and exercise. We studied what *"discernment"* means and how it relates to hearing the voice of God. Now, let's take a closer look at the diverse ways that God speaks to us.

IS THERE A SPECIFIC WAY GOD SPEAKS TO ME?

There are many ways that God speaks to us today. We will share three primary ways, which are common with most believers.

Isaiah 21:2-3 gives us these three different methods or ways we may perceive the voice of God or the way He communicates with us:

> "A grievous **vision** is declared to me; the treacherous one still deals treacherously, and the destroyer still destroys. Go up, O Elam. Lay siege, O Media. All her sighing I have made to cease. Therefore, **my loins are filled with pain**; pangs have taken hold of me as the pangs of a woman who travails. I am so perplexed at the **hearing** of it; I am so dismayed at the **seeing** of it." (Isaiah 21:2–3; MEV)

God primarily speaks to us through our natural senses in a supernatural way. He speaks to us through our Vision, Hearing and Feelings. Which of these is the primary way that you hear God? As you identify which what is your "frequency" like a radio searching for a station, you will be able to hear God more clearly.

Prophetic Revelation will and should be common in our day. Acts 2:17-18 says

> "'And in the last days it shall be, God declares, that I will pour out my Spirit on all flesh, and your sons and your daughters shall prophesy, and your young men shall see visions, and your old men

shall dream dreams; even on my male servants and female servants in those days I will pour out my Spirit, and they shall prophesy." (Acts 2:17–18; ESV)

VISIONS, DREAMS, PICTURES

Visions usually occur while you are awake; your spiritual eyes are opened supernaturally by God to see the spirit realm. Dreams occur during sleep, also called "night visions." At times, pictures or what is referred to as impressions, either in the mind or heart, are glimpses of revelation given by God to a person.

EXAMPLES OF VISIONS

"Then Elisha prayed and said, "O Lord, please open his eyes that he may see." So the Lord opened the eyes of the young man, and he saw, and behold, the mountain was full of horses and chariots of fire all around Elisha." (2 Kings 6:17; ESV)

"But he, full of the Holy Spirit, gazed into heaven and saw the glory of God, and Jesus standing at the right hand of God. And he said, "Behold, I see the heavens opened, and the Son of Man standing at the right hand of God.""" (Acts 7:55–56; ESV)

EXAMPLES OF DREAMS

"Daniel declared, "I saw in my vision by night, and behold, the four winds of heaven were stirring up the great sea." (Daniel 7:2; ESV)

"But as he considered these things, behold, an angel of the Lord appeared to him in a dream, saying, "Joseph, son of David, do not fear to take Mary as your wife, for that which is conceived in her is from the Holy Spirit." (Matthew 1:20; ESV)

WISDOM FOR DREAMS AND VISION

Mental Pictures — these are images, at times like photos that we can perceive in our mind and heart. You see this very commonly with the Prophets in the Old Testament.

One example is the Prophet Jeremiah; we see how God right at the beginning of His ministry began to not only speak to Him directly through His Voice but also visually. In this passage of Scripture, we see God not only asking Him *"What do you see?"* But God provides the interpretation of the pictures and visions he is seeing.

> "And the word of the Lord came to me, saying, "Jeremiah, what do you see?" And I said, "I see an almond branch." Then the Lord said to me, "You have seen well, for I am watching over my word to perform it." The word of the Lord came to me a second time, saying, "What do you see?" And I said, "I see a boiling pot, facing away from the north." Then the Lord said to me, "Out of the north disaster shall be let loose upon all the inhabitants of the land." (Jeremiah 1:11–14; ESV)

When you have visions and dreams, things may not always seem clear. They often can seem vague. At times, when God is trying to get a point across, you will see things pointedly highlighted or clear. But at times, you may feel like the symbolism of things is intimidating and hard to interpret; don't give up, and press in for God to show you what they mean.

We can see, for example, Prophet Ezekiel having a hard time describing his visions. We see him use words that are vague (like, appearance, likeness); comparing things he saw in the spirit to things in the natural in an effort to describe what he saw.

"As I looked, behold, a stormy wind came out of the north, and a great cloud, with brightness around it, and fire flashing forth continually, and in the midst of the fire, as it were gleaming metal. And from the midst of it came the likeness of four living creatures. And this was their appearance: they had a human likeness, but each had four faces, and each of them had four wings. Their legs were straight, and the soles of their feet were like the sole of a calf's foot. And they sparkled like burnished bronze. Under their wings on their four sides they had human hands. And the four had their faces and their wings thus: their wings touched one another. Each one of them went straight forward, without turning as they went." (Ezekiel 1:4–9, ESV)

The key to dreams and visions is asking God for wisdom and revelation, for interpretation and application. We frequently see in the Old Testament, Prophets asking God questions, inquiring of Him for revelation, interpretation, and application of what God was showing to them.

We see this happen with Prophet Daniel.

"'As for me, Daniel, my spirit within me was anxious, and the visions of my head alarmed me. I approached one of those who stood there and asked him the truth concerning all this. So he told me and made known to me the interpretation of the things." (Daniel 7:15–16; ESV)

Don't be anxious or alarmed about what you see in your visions or dreams. Ask God for help, and He will speak to you. God is interested in having a personal, interactive relationship with us, where we can ask questions and receive answers. He is also interested in us sharing with him, our concerns, ideas and yes even fears so He can help us overcome.

HEARING

We've looked at how God can speak visually to us. Now, let's take a closer look at how God can speak to us through hearing His voice.

> "And your ears shall hear a word behind you, saying, "This is the way, walk in it," when you turn to the right or when you turn to the left." (Isaiah 30:21; ESV)

Hearing the voice of God can come in many ways:
- Still small voice.
- Thoughts
- Audible Voice

These all come supernaturally as the Holy Spirit reveals to your mind, heart, and spirit. Because we have not been accustomed to hearing the voice of God, we can quickly dismiss slight impressions and thoughts from God. We must develop sensitivity to His voice.

In 1 Samuel 3, we see the story of the young prophet in training. Crucial times were upon Israel at that time, *"And the word of the Lord was rare in those days; there was no frequent vision"* (1 Samuel 3:1).

But God was training young Samuel to become a prophetic voice for such a time. The spiritual leadership of the day had begun to compromise. Eli, the priest, who represented the voice of God and the leadership of the day was old, it says that his *"eyesight had begun to grow dim so that he could not see, was lying down in his own place."* (1 Samuel 3:2) But *"The lamp of God had not yet gone out, and Samuel was lying down in the temple of the Lord, where the ark of God was."* (1 Samuel 3:3)

Here is the training that Samuel went through:

1 Samuel 3:4–10 (ESV) — Then the Lord called Samuel, and he said, "Here I am!" and ran to Eli and said, "Here I am, for you called me." But he said, "I did not call; lie down again." So he went and lay down. 6 And the Lord called again, "Samuel!" and Samuel arose and went to Eli and said, "Here I am, for you called me." But he said, "I did not call, my son; lie down again." Now Samuel did not yet know the Lord, and the word of the Lord had not yet been revealed to him. And the Lord called Samuel again the third time. And he arose and went to Eli and said, "Here I am, for you called me." Then Eli perceived that the Lord was calling the boy. Therefore Eli said to Samuel, "Go, lie down, and if he calls you, you shall say, 'Speak, Lord, for your servant hears.' " So Samuel went and lay down in his place. And the Lord came and stood, calling as at other times, "Samuel! Samuel!" And Samuel said, "Speak, for your servant hears."

Eli, although, spiritually lethargic and passive, was used of God to mentor and train Samuel. We can see how Samuel had to learn to become sensitive to the voice of God by obedience. We must not dismiss the small voice, thought, impression; by obedience, we will see fruit. We will develop our hearts, ears, and eyes to be sensitive to His voice and plans.

Notice that Samuel was in the Temple where the Ark of God was. This represents prayer and meditation. No great prophet or minister will ever reach the place of maturity outside of the presence of God.

There are many other examples, like Isaiah 6, not just hearing, but seeing the Glory of God.

FEELING

God will also speak to us through feelings. God created us after His image and likeness. He has emotions, just like we do; He feels things just like we do.

> Genesis 6:6 says "And the Lord regretted that he had made man on the earth, and it grieved him to his heart."

> Ephesians 4:30 "And do not grieve the Holy Spirit of God, by whom you were sealed for the day of redemption."

God has intense emotions and feelings towards us. His desires and plans are so great that He will do anything to love and wait for us to respond appropriately to Him.

> "In overflowing anger for a moment, I hid my face from you, but with everlasting love I will have compassion on you," says the Lord, your Redeemer." (Isaiah 54:8; ESV)

> "the Lord appeared to him from far away. I have loved you with an everlasting love; therefore I have continued my faithfulness to you." (Jeremiah 31:3; ESV)

How can God use our emotions, feelings, and physical body to speak?

Physical Pain— words of knowledge about healings.

Emotions— stress, anxiety, sadness, anger. Sometimes this works through discerning of spirits. Joy, peace, and sensing the presence of God.

EXAMPLES OF HEARING GOD THROUGH OUR FEELINGS & EMOTIONS

The Ministry of Jesus was marked by strong feelings of compassion for multitudes and individuals.

"When he went ashore he saw a great crowd, and he had compassion on them, because they were like sheep without a shepherd. And he began to teach them many things." (Mark 6:34; ESV)

"'I have compassion on the crowd, because they have been with me now three days and have nothing to eat." (Mark 8:2; ESV)

"'For you shall go out in joy and be led forth in peace; the mountains and the hills before you shall break forth into singing, and all the trees of the field shall clap their hands." (Isaiah 55:12; ESV)

OTHER WAYS GOD SPEAKS:

We can sometimes limit God, remember that He is Supernatural. He created the natural realm; it is subjected to the Supernatural. He invades time from an eternal realm to supernaturally speak to each of us. Every dream, vision, thoughts is the Supernatural God speaking to us in our Natural realm.

Isaiah 58:8-9 says "For my thoughts are not your thoughts, neither are your ways my ways, declares the Lord. For as the heavens are higher than the earth so are my ways higher than your ways and my thoughts than your thoughts."

In the next chapter, we will take a closer look at the specific gifts of the prophetic and how they manifest.

ACTIVATION

"Activations" are opportunities for you to stir up the gift of God inside of you.

2 Timothy 1:6–7 (ESV) — *For this reason I remind you to fan into flame the gift of God, which is in you through the laying* *on of my hands, for God gave us a spirit not of fear but of power and love and self-control.*

Through stirring or fanning into flame the gifts of God, we can exercise our senses to discern the voice of God.

Hebrews 5:14 (ESV) — *But solid food is for the mature, for those who have their powers of discernment trained by constant practice to distinguish good from evil.*

Activation: Prophesy to an Individual

Description: In this activation, put some worship music on, and ask God to speak to you a word for you. In this activation, ask God to show you something specific He wants to speak to you about. Again, it may come as a picture, word, thought or vision. If you would like to sing a song, go ahead and do that, if you would like to draw what you saw, go ahead and do that. Give the Holy Spirit the permission to speak to you and give yourself permission to hear Him speak to you.

_____
_____
_____
_____
_____
_____
_____
_____
_____
_____
_____
_____
_____
_____
_____
_____
_____

CHAPTER 5

THE PROPHETIC GIFTS

"Now I want you all to speak in tongues, but even more to prophesy. The one who prophesies is greater than the one who speaks in tongues, unless someone interprets, so that the church may be built up."

(1 Corinthians 14:5, ESV)

Spiritual gifts work. They actually produce effective ministry. When they do not, something is wrong with the Body's health. If the Bible is clear about anything, it is clear that (1) God wants every Christian to have and to use a spiritual gift or gifts and that (2) He wants His lost sheep to be found and His Church to grow. Spiritual gifts are utilitarian. They are functional. They have a task to do, and if they are working properly, the task will be accomplished. When the gifts work together in a church that wants to grow and the church is willing to pay the price for growth, the church will see God's blessing, and it should grow because it will be healthy.

C. Peter Wagner

Your Spiritual Gifts: Can Help Your Church Grow

Before we dive into the gifts, I would like to emphasize the importance and role the Holy Spirit plays in gracing each one of us with diverse gifts and ways of being used for God's Glory.

> "There are different kinds of spiritual gifts, but the same Spirit is the source of them all. There are different kinds of service, but we serve the same Lord. God works in different ways, but it is the same God who does the work in all of us. A spiritual gift is given to each of us so we can help each other." (1 Corinthians 12:4–7; NLT)

First, it's important to know that a person with the gift of healing is not better than the person with the gift of prophecy. The Holy Spirit is the same source of each gift. We have distinct ways that we serve in the Kingdom. The importance and priority of the gifts are the fact that it's *"given to each of us so we can help each other."* Another translation says, *"to produce what is beneficial."*

If your ministry is not producing benefits for the Body of Christ to expand and move into its fullness of purpose, then you may need to check and allow the Holy Spirit to mold you into His instrument fit for the Kingdom. Let's bear good fruit for the Kingdom!

Secondly, *"...the gifts and the calling of God are irrevocable" (Romans 11:29; ESV)*. If the Holy Spirit is the "source" of every spiritual gift (supernatural ability) given to us, and these gifts are "irrevocable," it is our responsibility to steward, cultivate and grow in them. It's very important for you to understand that your gift was active in your life whether it was in your unredeemed nature in your past or your redeemed nature now—you were gifted by God, and it's time to discover that gift and learn to use it.

VOCAL GIFTS (PROPHETIC GIFTS)

Here is a brief list of the vocal gifts taken from 1 Corinthians 12:4-7. The reason we refer to these as "vocal" is because they communicate God's mind, will and heart through speaking and hearing.

- Word of Knowledge
- Word of Wisdom
- Discernment of Spirits
- Prophecy
- Speaking in Tongues
- Interpretation of Tongues

WORD OF KNOWLEDGE

A word of knowledge is a supernatural revelation of the Holy Spirit to you of specific facts that come from the mind of God for another person. These facts are accurate and give information about the past, present, or future of a person. Word of Knowledge can bring revelation about a person for a specific situation, and these details can bring clarity and specifics to their situations. This is not limited to one person; it can happen in business, church, city or nation.

The purpose of the word of knowledge is to reveal—either problems or roots of these problems, strongholds, mindsets causing delay to spiritual growths, illnesses or expose demonic possession. Many times, it can reveal information about family situations some have experienced where God will reveal where things are that have been lost or stolen.

USES OF WORD OF KNOWLEDGE IN SCRIPTURE

Dick Iverson, says in his book, *The Holy Spirit Today*, that there are six ways in which scripture shows the operation of the Word of Knowledge:

- Knowledge of the thoughts of men's hearts - Luke 6:8; 7:36-50; Matthew 3:7-12.
- Knowledge of men's plans or motives -1 Kings 21:17-20 and Luke 6:8.
- Knowledge of facts of the past, present or future - John 11:11-16; Acts 11:27-30.
- Knowledge of the whereabouts of men - 1 Samuel 10:1-24; Acts 9:10-18; Acts 10:19; Acts 16:9-10.
- Knowledge to warn of coming danger - 2
- Kings 6:9; Acts 20:28-30.
- Knowledge to expose hypocrisy or deception- 2 Kings 5:20-27; 1 Kings 4; Acts 5:1-10.

WORD OF WISDOM

It's one of the Holy Spirit's gifts or supernatural ability that gives special revelation and specific instruction, guidance or advice. Many times, this revelation brings solutions to insurmo-untable problems; it brings life-changing wisdom to a person and situation.

This word implies something of the future, and it brings revelation regarding people, events, and situations. It brings strategy and implementation. The word of wisdom can work with the word of knowledge, bringing strategy to implement the revelation that was revealed.

Some purposes are to warn and to prevent events, to confirm and affirm a calling. Word of Wisdom can be used to give guidance and counsel to business people, to Government officials, etc. There are many ways this gift can manifest, the importance here is to profit the body of Christ, in other words, to build it up!

DISCERNMENT OF SPIRITS

It is the supernatural ability to discern what spirit is operating in a person, situation, behaviors, and circumstances.
THERE ARE THREE KINDS OF SPIRITS:
- **Human** - Behavior, motivations, etc.
- **Satanic** - Demons, principalities, strengths, etc..
- **Divine** - Holy Spirit, Joy, Peace, Spirit of Praise, Worship, Prophetic, Wisdom, etc.

Some of the purposes of Discerning of spirits is to discern strongholds, principalities, demonic oppression in your life, family, business, city, etc. You can discern the human spirit that causes a person to have certain attitudes or ways of thinking. Sometimes, we can discern the works of the flesh vs. the works of demonic spirits.

This gift is very useful in ministering deliverance, to bring freedom to an individual, church or region. If you are a pastor of a local church, you can sometimes discern in your services when God wants to move with healing and miracles, deliverance or prophecy.

PROPHECY

The Gift of Prophecy is the supernatural ability by the Holy Spirit to hear God's heart and thoughts to share with someone else. This gift often reveals destiny, purpose, God's plans, and desires for others.

The purpose of the prophetic word is always for edification, exhortation, and comfort.

EDIFY

Through the gift of prophecy, you can edify or build a person. This is crucial in the family as parents are called to build up their children, which in this case, a prophetic word can do that. Every prophetic word always edifies a person; it causes them to be drawn to a more and intimate relationship with the Lord. It matures them in their relationship. When we prophesy, we begin to bring words that build a person, and words that promote their growth and maturity in Christ. Your prophetic word can be another brick needed to build a believer's life and promote them to the next place of fruitfulness in the Lord.

EXHORTATION

To exhort here means an encouragement, for strengthening and establishing the believer in faith. To call someone near and call them to the place they can get help (a word that refreshes them). When we release a word of exhortation inspired by the Holy Spirit, it will bring out the above fruit in a person, church or family.

COMFORT

To console, encouragement. The Greek (paramuthia) word here expresses a greater degree of tenderness, at least by word of mouth than exhortation (paraklesis). In other words, this word brings peace, calm, persuasion of comfort in times of crisis or need.

All these are done through the revelation of the Holy Spirit, as every word is inspired by the Spirit of God and given by you, allowing God to use you to edify, exhort and comfort.

SPEAKING IN TONGUES AND INTERPRETATION OF TONGUES

This is the supernatural ability given by the Holy Spirit to speak in various heavenly tongues; it's a direct communication with the Spirit of God, something that cannot be understood human wise, but the supernatural ability of interpretation is given by the Spirit of God to interpret what we are praying in the Spirit.

One of the purposes of our heavenly language is to build ourselves (1 Corinthians 14:4 and Jude 1:20). This is one of the most powerful secrets that all prophetic ministers need to know. Speaking in tongues strengthens us and builds us up and prepares us to minister with power and authority.

EXERCISING THE GIFTS OF THE HOLY SPIRIT

Now that you have a definition of the Prophetic or Revelatory Gifts of the Holy Spirit, I want to give you some guidelines and practical tips in exercising your spiritual gift.

HOW CAN WE ACTIVATE THE GIFTS OF THE HOLY SPIRIT?

"For this reason I remind you to fan into flame the gift of God, which is in you through the laying on of my hands" (2 Timothy 1:6, ESV).

The Apostle Paul exhorts Timothy to revive the gifts of God which are in him. One of the ways that we activate the gifts is through faith. Faith is trust in Gods faithfulness.

When we activate our gift, we are trusting Gods faithfulness that He has given us something beneficial for His Body.

An example is speaking in tongues, if you are a born again believer you can be spirit filled and receive the gift of speaking in tongues. A great resource for you is 70 Reasons for Speaking in Tongues by Dr. Bill Hamon, I highly recommend you read it. For the purpose of this explanation I will assume you already speak in tongues, answer the following questions to help you understand:

- Begin to speak in tongues, building yourself up according to scripture in your most Holy Faith (Jude 20). Now the question is, can you speak in tongues whenever and wherever you desire?
- The second question is, did you force the Holy Spirit to speak in tongues?

No! The word of God says that the gift is given to all according to His will and it is exercised through faith.

One of the restored truths of the Prophetic Movement is the revelation to activate and train every member of the Body of Christ in the gifts of the Holy Spirit. We should practice activations with the goal to activate the spiritual gifts in the believer.

An activation is an exercise so that the believer receives and manifests the grace to do what the Bible says we are to do. It awakens, activates, revives and frees the abilities of God in the saints.

When Paul exhorts Timothy to revive his gift, he was telling him: "BE JEALOUS, FULL OF ZEAL AND DESIRE TO EXERCISE YOUR GIFT, REVIVING THE GIFT OF GOD IN YOUR LIFE." In verse 7, it says: For

God has not given us a spirit of fear and timidity but of power, love, and self-discipline.

During the activations, you can exercise your gift without fear. God did not give us a spirit of fear but of power, love, and self-discipline. If you make a mistake, it does not matter because that is what activations are for, to learn from our mistakes. This is an opportunity to learn and exercise your gift. So that when you go out into the streets or minister in a prophetic team, it is no longer time to practice or activate; it is time to ACT!

OUR SPIRITUAL LANGUAGE OUR POWER GENERATOR

Jude 1:20 says: But you, dear friends, must build each other up in your most holy faith, pray in the power of the Holy Spirit.

Corinthians 14:4 says: He who speaks in a tongue edifies himself. The word edifies means to repair, build an hour, build from a foundation, to be founded, established, promote spiritual growth, divine grace, virtue, holiness, blessing, and power.

When you speak in tongues, you are edifying your spirit so that the spiritual gifts can flow through you. You are being grounded and established in your gifts, in your destiny and calling in God. The grace of God flows without obstacle, and His power can flow freely through you.

The gift of speaking in tongues is the gift of the Holy Spirit in us for our edification and preparation in the ministry.

CHAPTER 6

OLD AND NEW ROADMAPS PROPHETS TODAY

"But now the righteousness of God has been manifested apart from the law, although the Law and the Prophets bear witness to it—"

(Romans 3:21, ESV)

Under the new covenant we don't usually see prophets who live by themselves in the wilderness. The prophetic ministry is a vital part of the body of Christ in a city. Prophetic people are mandated by Scripture to be involved in the local church, not separated from it. Prophetic people serve within the church as one of the "joints that supply" the other parts of the church, enabling it to be the prophetic voice in the earth (Eph. 4:16).

Mike Bickle

Growing in the Prophetic

63

The Prophetic Movement accelerated after the late 1980s as Dr. Bill Hamon and Christian International focused their efforts to bring a proper and balanced understanding of the role of the Prophet and prophetic movement. Even though it's been almost 30 years since the prophetic was launched, there are emerging prophetic voices that have not received the proper training and understanding of Present Truth regarding New Testament Prophets and Prophetic Ministry.

By its nature, a prophetic culture (values, standards, what is acceptable or not, etc...) is the result of the beliefs and values that prophets and prophetic ministries uphold. For over 50 years, Christian International has been pioneering a better way to do prophetic ministry, culture, and training for the Saints and Prophets. Dr. Bill Hamon says that of all the fivefold ministries, *I believe prophets need training in wisdom and proper practice of their ministry the most.* Dr. Bill Hamon (Prophets and Prophetic Movement)

Prophets need wisdom and training because we represent the intimate voice of God to nations, families, and saints. We have the ability to adequately express the voice of God that can affirm, heal and restore or can destroy and hurt the eternal purpose of God over people. Dr. Bill Hamon compares the power of a prophetic word released as a laser that can heal and restore or bring harm and death:

> "God's armory of weapons and means of ministry, few others, I be-
> lieve, have as great a potential for blessing or devastation as proph-
> ecy. Like the laser, it can be used to bring life, healing, and restora-
> tion; or confusion, disruption, and death. Prophecy is no play toy.
> God has not given it merely to satisfy the curious."

> Dr. Bill Hamon *(Prophets and Personal Prophecy)*

For this reason, we need to understand the function and expression of a New Testament Prophet today. Every saint lives the Christian life according to the revelation they have of God, the Kingdom, and His Principles. Prophets and prophetic ministers function and express their prophetic ministry in the same manner. The culture that ministries express is a by-product of the values that are celebrated, and those values are determined by the revelation that they have about God and His Word. What determines a successful prophet and ministry is that they are wise to examine themselves considering God's whole counsel of His Word and Spirit.

I will say, from the beginning, that each one has a unique personality and by that, I mean the way we naturally tend to express, feel and perceive God and His voice. Some of the personality traits we have are aligned with God's nature and personality, but some must be surrendered and put to death so we may obtain His nature in fullness to live a life worthy of His Kingdom.

OLD ROADMAP | OLD DESTINATION

> The prophets must be made knowledgeable of the many pitfalls they must avoid. It is not enough to fill the car with gas to go; the driver must be given driving instructions and a road map if he or she is to use the vehicle properly and reach the desired destination.
>
> Dr. Bill Hamon *(Prophets and the Prophetic Movement)*

In our advanced technological world, we find our roadmaps in our cell phones. This has allowed us to have the latest updates to the best directions to our destinations. In the said manner, it's time for emerging prophetic ministers to update their prophetic GPS and for some, it may require an upgrade for them to enter into the fullness of the purpose of God for their life.

I often find myself hearing prophetic ministers use Old Testament Prophets as models for New Testament Prophets. There is nothing wrong with gleaning from how prophets functioned in the Old Testament, it has its benefits, but it has its pitfalls that can be dangerous. Scriptures ask us to take the "patience" of prophets as our example, not their prophetic ministry and style (James 5:10). A wounded and unhealed prophetic voice can easily identify with the ministry style and weight of the Old Testament message.

We sometimes refer to this as "doom and gloom." I don't personally believe God is a "doom and gloom" God, His goodness and steadfast love are everlasting. Hebrews 1:1 declares: "Long ago, at many times and in many ways, God spoke to our fathers by the prophets," God has used every way possible to communicate and speak directly to His people and sometimes it was through His severity that He was able to draw them back to His Goodness.

> "Note then the kindness and the severity of God: severity toward those who have fallen, but God's kindness to you, provided you continue in his kindness. Otherwise you too will be cut off. And even they, if they do not continue in their unbelief, will be grafted in, for God has the power to graft them in again." (Romans 11:22–23; ESV)

We must take note of both His kindness and severity, not just His severity. I mentioned earlier a wounded and unhealed prophetic voice could easily fall into the pitfall of believing their ministry is like that of an Old Testament Prophet, misunderstanding that often, God provided prophets to nations and people who had been rebellious, worshiped other idols and become self-absorbed. It's a terrible way to find a job description for New Testament Prophet based on Old Testament dispensa-tions alone.

I want to be careful, because by no means do I believe that God will not use judgment, correction, and rebuke as an instrument of justice, and I will go as far to say as an instrument of His love, I believe He does, and He continues to till today. But is it our function as prophets today primarily that of speaking judgment, pointing the finger at every weakness and deficiency in the Body of Christ? I don't believe so.

Prophetic Ministry Expressions are born from the roadmap we have chosen to follow, one leads to an old destination, while the other leads to the new destination we are called into. The old covenant served its purpose and Jesus came to fulfill its purpose and establish a new and better covenant. Hebrews 8:6-7 declares that the work of the New Testament Church and Ministers is much greater and important than the one that was done under the Old Covenant.

> "But as it is, Christ has obtained a ministry that is as much more excellent than the old as the covenant he mediates is better, since it is enacted on better promises. For if that first covenant had been faultless, there would have been no occasion to look for a second." (Hebrews 8:6–7, ESV)

The covenant that Jesus mediates and has entrusted to us is better. Offering salvation, transformation and freedom in Him. The prophetic promises that are released in our day, through the Holy Spirit carry within them the power to launch us into our Destiny as we believe them. I decclare: You are a New Covenant Prophetic Minister.

OLD TESTAMENT PROPHETS
FUNCTION VS. EXPRESSION

There is a clear difference between function and expression of the prophets and prophetic ministry. *Function* speaks of the *role, job description, and task*. *Expression,* on the other hand, is directly linked to the *personality and character of the individual*. It is clear in the Scripture that Prophets have a call (function) to govern, lead and guide as part of God's established Government that serves the Body of Christ.

Many of the Old Testament functions as appointed overseers of nations, spokesman on behalf of God to His people, leaders, and guides among Kings are still operating today. We must take careful note of how they functioned because of the dispensation they lived in their day. In the Old Testament, everything was filtered through the law. Prophets had a unique call to point Israel and nations to the Laws of God, which gave a glimpse and path to the coming Messiah.

"But now the righteousness of God has been manifested apart from the law, although the Law and the Prophets bear witness to it— the righteousness of God through faith in Jesus Christ for all who believe. For there is no distinction:" (Romans 3:21–22, ESV)

The Prophets and the Law bear witness of Christ and reveal to us one of the primary functions that Old Testament Prophets had, which was to guide, direct and point towards the coming Messiah. Going back to Hebrews 1:1, God spoke through the Prophets in numerous ways and many times directing the people with expectation towards the Messiah. When Jesus came into the scene, verse two declares *"but in these last days he has spoken to us by his Son, whom he appointed the heir of all things, through whom also he created the world."* (Hebrews 1:2)

The New Testament Prophet function has not changed from the Old Testament, we now direct, guide and point towards the Second Coming of Christ, but there was an added dimension that must be properly understood to balance the ministry of the prophetic in the last days. If the prophet predominantly focuses on Old Testament Functions of his ministry today, he misses the most critical role and function He has in the current dispensation we live in—a dispensation of grace and mercy in preparing a Bride for Christ.

Just as Old Testament Prophets filtered their ministry, calling and functions through the Law, we as Present-Truth, New Testament Prophets must now filter everything through the Righteousness that has been revealed through Christ Jesus Himself, which is apart from the Law. By no means does this mean pick up your Bible and take out the Old Testament. It means, there must be a renewal of the mind and baptism into the new and better covenant that speaks a better word (Hebrews 12:24).

A classic example of the prophetic whose function and expression were closely aligned with Heaven's principles and culture was Daniel. During captivity, He became the overseer of the affairs of a Kingdom and Prophetic Intercessor for a people captive at the tipping point of freedom (Daniel 2:46-49; Daniel 9-12).

> "There is a man in your kingdom in whom is the Spirit of the Holy God. And, in the days of your father, light and understanding and wisdom, like the wisdom of the gods, were found in him. And King Nebuchadnezzar, your father, your father the king, made him master of the magicians, astrologers, Chaldeans, and soothsayers. Inasmuch as an excellent spirit and knowledge and understanding, interpreting dreams and explanation of enigmas and solving of

> problems, were found in the same Daniel, whom the king named Belteshazzar, now let Daniel be called, and he will give the interpretation."" (Daniel 5:11–12; MEV)

Having God's favor along with an excellent spirit, wisdom and understanding is the key to healthy prophets and prophetic ministry.

Expression of prophetic ministries are linked to the personality and character of an individual. It is imperative to understand the difference between the function of old covenant prophets versus new covenant (more on that later) because personality can amplify the role in a healthy manner or detrimental way.

One classic example of an old covenant prophet whose personality and character dangerously amplified his function was Jonah.

Jonah, a prophet called to bring a word that would cause a revival of repentance upon the people had an unstable personality and character flaw that amplified his function in a disadvantageous way. He ran away from God and secondly, once he obeyed God, he became angry at the result because his personality and character did not want to align to God's compassion and mercy (Jonah 4:1–11).

Now that we have examined how function and expression work closely together, we will study the New Testament Function and Expression of a Prophet. Declare this prayer with me: *Father God, I thank you that as I renew my mind through your word, my prophetic ministry, voice and, character align with your transforming power!*

NEW ROADMAP | NEW DESTINATION

HIS BODY & HIS BRIDE

One of the most significant and radical changes that took place as we transitioned from the Old Covenant to the New Covenant was the birth of the Ekklesia, The Body of Christ, The Bride of Jesus. God utterly erased the divide between a chosen nation and the rest of humanity. He established a Body through His Son that would become His Son's Bride. A bride that rules and governs with authority and power, with mercy and compassion, with grace and justice.

With this radical transition came a better way, a more excellent way for God's release of His Kingdom upon Earth. And this very change is the most radical transition Prophets must undergo. God spoke to me a revelation that truly transformed my prophetic ministry; He said to me,

> "You are not just ministering to a group of saints and believers, you are literally ministering to My Son's Bride, His Body!" I had a heart transformation take place at that very moment. I could no longer see my ministry as a prophet, as just prophesying to believers and saints. Jesus has allowed His 5-fold ministers to help prepare His Bride and Body for His Second Coming.

When Paul needed to exhort husbands on how they should love their wives, he used Jesus as the example and standard. It is the same standard I believe we must hold onto as ministers:

> "And you husbands, show the same kind of love to your wives as Christ showed to the Church when he died for her, to make her holy and clean, washed by baptism and God's Word; so that he could give her to himself as a glorious Church without a single spot or wrinkle or any other blemish, being holy and without a single fault. That is how husbands should treat their wives, loving them

71

as parts of themselves. For since a man and his wife are now one, a man is really doing himself a favor and loving himself when he loves his wife! No one hates his own body but lovingly cares for it, just as Christ cares for his body the Church, of which we are parts. (That the husband and wife are one body is proved by the Scripture, which says, "A man must leave his father and mother when he marries so that he can be perfectly joined to his wife, and the two shall be one.") I know this is hard to understand, but it is an illustration of the way we are parts of the body of Christ. So again I say, a man must love his wife as a part of himself; and the wife must see to it that she deeply respects her husband—obeying, praising, and honoring him." (Ephesians 5:25–33; The Living Bible)

As Prophets, we are the very expression of the Voice of Jesus to His Bride. The question we should ask ourselves is, would we speak to our spouse the way we speak to the Body of Christ? I believe some will cringe as you read this because with our words, we beat down the Bride of Jesus. Could it be possible that we have bruised the soul of the Church? Dangerously slowed down her growth and maturity because we reveal only inadequacies instead of speaking life and destiny to her?

This is the foundation of a New Testament Prophets standard and the basis for expression of ministry and culture. The Bride of Christ is beautiful even with all her imperctions, Jesus still loves Her!

With this in mind, let's examine the function of a New Testament Prophet.

NEW TESTAMENT FUNCTIONS OF A PROPHET

Ephesians 4:11-14 gives us a clear description of the function or job description of a New Testament Prophet.

*"And he gave the apostles, the prophets, the evangelists, the shepherds and teachers, **to equip the saints** for the work of ministry, **for building up the body of Christ**, until we all attain to the unity of the faith and of the knowledge of the Son of God, to mature manhood, to the measure of the stature of the fullness of Christ, so that we may no longer be children, tossed to and fro by the waves and carried about by every wind of doctrine, by human cunning, by craftiness in deceitful schemes."* (Ephesians 4:11–14; ESV)

EQUIP AND BUILD

The primary function of New Testament prophets is to equip and build the Body of Christ. There are many prophets who love prophesying, and God has given them an anointing to release personal prophetic ministry. There are prophets whose primary prophetic ministry expression is in government or business. But no matter where that ministry is expressed, their job description still includes equipping and building. Who are they called to equip and build? The Body of Christ, His Bride.

HOW DO YOU EQUIP?

Ephesians 4:11 says that the primary reason why Christ has given prophets to the Body of Christ is to equip His Body for the work of the ministry. Prophets today, have a desire not only to prophesy but to equip the saints by activating the gifts of the Holy Spirit and properly teaching them how to use them.

The word *katartismos* in Greek means

*"**adequacy**, complete furnishing, a preparation or training that fully qualifies"* James Swanson (Dictionary of Biblical Languages)

to make someone completely adequate or sufficient for something—'to make adequate, to furnish completely, to cause to be fully qualified, adequacy.' Johannes P. Louw and Eugene Albert Nida (Greek-English Lexicon of the New Testament)

Prophets have an anointing to help the Body of Christ prepare through training, to help them reach the standard that qualifies them for proper ministry work. Dr. Bill Hamon says

> Classical Pentecostals and Charismatics believe they can biblically educate someone about the Holy Spirit baptism and then help pray that person through to speaking in tongues. They will even give them step-by-step instructions and acts of faith to take to activate the Holy Spirit gift of their own prayer and praise language.
>
> In a similar way, the Prophetic Movement is bringing the revelation knowledge, methods, ways and means of teaching, activating and maturing saints in their gifts of the Holy Spirit and spiritual ministries.
>
> Dr. Bill Hamon (Prophets and the Prophetic Movement)

When Prophets are properly functioning in the Body of Christ, there is a release of the Father's Voice among the Saints that can encourage, exhort and comfort (1 Corinthians 14:3).

HOW DO YOU BUILD?

I find it interesting that the Apostle Paul does not focus on much on the equipping part in this passage and focuses primarily in what building the Body of Christ will look like. He specifically says that building will result in:

- Unity of the Faith
- Knowledge of the Son of God
- Maturity to the measure and stature of the Fullness of Christ

- Protection from Doctrinal Winds created by man, due to their cunning ways and crafty, deceitful schemes.

Building up means to help the Body of Christ grow in maturity. The UBS Handbook says that *"to build up can be translated in some languages by "caused to grow" or "caused to grow strong."* Robert G. Bratcher and Eugene Albert Nida.

When a prophet is functioning and properly positioned in the Body of Christ, he has an anointing to help bring the Body of Christ to maturity.

CHAPTER 7

THE MIRACULOUS POWER OF THE PROPHETIC WORD

"Then Elijah, the prophet from Tishbe in Gilead, told King Ahab, "As surely as the Lord God of Israel lives—the God whom I worship and serve—there won't be any dew or rain for several years until I say the word!""

(1 Kings 17:1, The Living Bible)

I have found that when God speaks, a new kind of faith is released—I call it untried faith. This is simple to understand, and the Scriptures define it in the New Testament Book of James: "...Faith without works is dead" (James 2:20). So if your faith has not worked for you, it is dead. Once you have tried that faith, and it has worked, it is quite realistically "known" faith. You become familiar with it, and in fact, you use that faith to touch and help other people.

Kim Clement

Call Me Crazy, But I'm Hearing God

1 Kings 17:1, it says: *"Now Elijah the Tishbite, of Tishbe in Gilead, said to Ahab, "As the Lord, the God of Israel, lives, before whom I stand, there shall be neither dew nor rain these years, except by my word.""* (1 Kings 17:1; ESV)

Is it possible that the word of the Prophet or the prophetic minister could have such power, enough to cause a drought to demonstrate the miraculous power of God? Prophetic words do not only reveal destiny and purpose, but each word brings with it the miraculous power of God to bind and loose, open and close, proclaim and declare the power of God.

The reason we do not witness more miraculous manifestations, deliverances and souls being saved through the gifts of the Holy Spirit is because we lack boldness and faith in its power. The Prophet Elijah had to believe what he heard when he released the word, and the people believed. This caused miracles in the natural when it was impossible.

The Prophet Elijah was sent by God after declaring this word to a widow that only had a *"handful"* of dough for her and her son to eat. After that, they would die from lack of food, but the Prophet declared another Prophetic word amid the negative word that had shut the heavens. Verse 10b-16 says:

> "10 So he arose and went to Zarephath. And when he came to the gate of the city, behold, a widow was there gathering sticks. And he called to her and said, "Bring me a little water in a vessel, that I may drink." 11 And as she was going to bring it, he called to her and said, "Bring me a morsel of bread in your hand." 12 And she said, "As the Lord your God lives, I have nothing baked, only a handful of flour in a jar and a little oil in a jug. And now I am gathering a couple of sticks that I may go in and prepare it for myself and my son, that we may eat it and die." 13 And Elijah said to her, "Do not fear; go and do as you have said. But first make me a little cake of it and bring it to me, and afterward make something for yourself

and your son. 14 For thus says the Lord, the God of Israel, 'The jar of flour shall not be spent, and the jug of oil shall not be empty, until the day that the Lord sends rain upon the earth.' " 15 And she went and did as Elijah said. And she and he and her household ate for many days. 16 The jar of flour was not spent, neither did the jug of oil become empty, according to the word of the Lord that he spoke by Elijah.

What would have happened if Prophet Elijah wouldn't have declared that prophetic word in the widows' life? Majority of the time, we give up at the first negative response we receive or sense of opposition we face in life. It is time to prophesy that everything will change in your life. When the bank says "No," God says "I have a plan for your life." When you're fired from your job, God says "I have a new door opened for you." God's word has an untapped miraculous power that we have not experienced at its fullness.

RESURRECTION POWER
THE WORD OF GOD IS LIFE

"After this the son of the woman, the mistress of the house, became ill. And his illness was so severe that there was no breath left in him." (1 Kings 17:17; ESV)

After witnessing this miracle of abundance, we see that Prophet Elijah and the widows' faith is tested once again. The widows' son became ill and died. The widow started to blame the Prophet saying: *"What do you have against me, man of God? Did you come to remind me of my sin and kill my son?"*

In this occasion, the Prophet does not give a prophetic word that the son will be resurrected. Instead, the Prophet takes his place as an intercessor. This is a powerful example of the Prophet, minister or leader that is surrendered to their function and role as God's instrument. He did not shout "This is what the Lord says..." instead he took the boy to his room, and starts to cry out to God;

> "And he cried to the Lord, "O Lord my God, have you brought calamity even upon the widow with whom I sojourn, by killing her son?" Then he stretched himself upon the child three times and cried to the Lord, "O Lord my God, let this child's life come into him again." And the Lord listened to the voice of Elijah. And the life of the child came into him again, and he revived. And Elijah took the child and brought him down from the upper chamber into the house and delivered him to his mother. And Elijah said, "See, your son lives."" (1 Kings 17:20–23; ESV)

PROPHETIC INTERCESSORS

The prophet without prayer and intercession will see little success and fruitfulness. It's important to understand that personal prophecy is conditional. Meaning they require a heart, mind and will alignment from our part for them to be fulfilled. Sometimes, we put the weight on *"Thus says the Lord..."* than the very instructions God has given to us in that personal prophecy that can unlock the manifestation of the promise.

Prophetic Intercessors have a very important calling to intercede on behalf of others for the promises of God. Many believers in churches have dreams and promises that have not come to pass, and they have simply given up.

A prophetic intercessor has the anointing to resurrect the promises and dreams of God in the people. In my life, I have seen this happen. The dreams, visions, and the purpose of the ministries in my family seemed as if they would never come to pass. For a certain time, I gave these revelations up for dead, but when the anointing of prophetic intercession began to flow, I could see the miracles occurring in my family.

THE WORD OF KNOWLEDGE
THE MIRACLES, DELIVERANCE AND THE GOSPEL

2 Kings 5:1-27 relates the miracle of Naaman, the leper. Prophet Elisha through a word of knowledge tells him to wash in the Jordan River seven times. After Naaman had been healed, he offered Elisha a payment, but the prophet refused it. Prophet Elisha's helper, Gehazi, received the payment in secret and hid it. Through a word of knowledge, Prophet Elisha revealed Gehazi's sin and declared judgment over him. This is a crucial lesson; we should not use our gifts to obtain riches or prestige. Our motives should be right and pure before God.

In the end, through a Word of Knowledge inspired by the Holy Spirit, we can give instructions and direction that can bring healing as Prophet Elisha did for Naaman. It's important to note that a Word of Knowledge is not only to provide instructions and directions but can sometimes at its most basic function be to reveal a sickness in order to believe for the healing.

In 2 Kings 6:8-12 tells the story of how to the king of Syria warred against Israel. He was trying to ambush the land of Israel. The plans of the King of Syria were interrupted by Prophet Elisha who would warn the Israelites of the kings' plans. This infuriated the king, and he grew suspicious that someone in his land was a spy and summoned his servants. The servants responded it is the Prophet Elisha who tells the Israelites the plans of the King. A word of knowledge can reveal not only the strategy of the enemy towards an individual but can also show his position and the demons behind those attacks.

In John 4:18, 19-29, tells when Jesus came across a Samaritan woman at a well. Jesus told her, through a word of knowledge details of her life. This convinced the woman that Jesus is the Messiah. Not only did she believe but also trumpeted the news that Jesus was the Messiah throughout the town. Many became saved through a word of knowledge, which revealed the heart of a woman.

DISCERNMENT OF SPIRITS DELIVERANCE

In Mark 9:14-29, we see that a father brought his son to be delivered because he was oppressed by an unclean spirit. The disciples are trying to cast out the spirit when Jesus sees that they are arguing and attempting every method that could have possibly existed at the time. Jesus, through discernment of spirits, discerned that it is not the method that is failing, nor a wrong diagnosis, but rather unbelief. A careful reading of this passage reveals that Jesus emphasizes the need of faith to bring deliverance to the child. The diagnosis of demonic oppression was clear, the method was a simple command, but what was lacking was faith. Later, the disciples asked Jesus why they could not cast the demon out. Jesus response was that they needed prayer and fasting.

We see another example in Acts 16:16-18 when the Apostle Paul discerned a spirit of divination in a young slave girl. He rebuked the spirit, and she was set free.

HOW TO FLOW IN THE MIRACULOUS POWER OF PROPHETIC DECREES?

The power of a prophetic promise is activated through faith, but also a faith that believes that God wants to use us to release and receive those prophetic promises. One of the obstacles that hold us back from releasing prophetic words is that we try to understand it, the word is not for us but someone else. We are only the messengers, and our job is to release the word and let God do the rest. Have faith in God's faithfulness and His faithfulness to use you for His Glory.

Faith requires risk, total dependency on God. Matthew 11:12b *"the kingdom of heaven suffers violence, and the violent take it by force."* Prophetic ministry requires risk, men of violence willing to trust in the Holy Spirit. We can give birth to words which bring miracles that transform people, cities, and nations.

PRACTICAL POINTS:

- Cultivate a deep, passionate and intimate relationship with the Holy Spirit.
- Edify yourself by speaking in your spiritual language. God desires to give you power, and one of the ways that we access that power is through building ourselves up in our most Holy Faith, speaking in tongues.

- *"But you will receive power when the Holy Spirit has come upon you, and you will be my witnesses in Jerusalem and in all Judea and Samaria, and to the end of the earth.""* (Acts 1:8; ESV)
- *"But you, beloved, building yourselves up in your most holy faith and praying in the Holy Spirit,"* (Jude 20; ESV)

- Be open to divine appointments. If you do not seek and desire these appointments, you will not see them.
- Do not *neglect* to prophesy. When was the last time you gave a prophetic word to a friend or coworker? Go for it! Don't limit yourself to church, do it in the store, at work, school. You don't have to say, "This is what the Lord has said..." Simply share a thought.
  - Many times, it is as simple as asking a question. If you sense from the Lord that a person's children are in need, you could ask them "How their children are doing?" This could open the door for you to pray and bless them.

ACTIVATION:

Write down 3 personal situations in which you need to see a miracle of God. Pray that God will reveal what is holding back His release. Ask God for a word of wisdom, knowledge or discernment:

1._____

_____

_____

_____

_____

_____

_____

_____

2._____

_____

_____

_____

_____

_____

_____

_____

3._____

_____

_____

_____

_____

_____

_____

_____

CHAPTER 8

HOW CAN I DEVELOP MY SPIRITUAL GIFT?

"Guard well the splendid, God-given ability you received as a gift from the Holy Spirit who lives within you."

(2 Timothy 1:14, The Living Bible)

Growing in the prophetic requires that we accept the foundational truth that everyone who is born again is able function in simple prophecy. It is the will of God for everyone who loves Jesus to prophesy. This really is the inheritance of every born-again believer.

Mike Bickle

Growing in the Prophetic

DESIRE AND VALUE PROPHECY

P ursue love, and earnestly desire the spiritual gifts,
especially that you may prophesy" (1 Corinthians
14:1; ESV).

Scripture clearly gives us the freedom to desire spiritual
gifts and especially to be used of God to prophetically release destiny and purpose over the Body of Christ. This is
not something we should shy away from or neglect.

"Do not despise prophecies" (1 Thessalonians 5:20; ESV).
The Apostle Paul also encouraged us to not look down upon
prophetic ministry. We are to desire to prophesy, and we are
to allow the operation of prophetic ministry in our families
and churches.

When we despise prophetic ministry, we also lose the
desire to be used by God to prophesy. Value precedes desire, a greater understanding and revelation of prophets,
prophetic ministry will bring a greater manifestation of it
along with its benefits. Do you value prophetic ministry?
Do you honor God's office of the Prophet by welcoming
their ministry and function?

I often get asked, *"How can I develop my spiritual gift?"* I
have a lot of admiration for the people who have a fervent
desire to learn and grow in their spiritual lives. These are
people with hunger and thirst to be used by God. Now, to
give you an adequate answer, I must touch two important
points. First of all, the qualities a person must possess in
order to grow in the kingdom of God and second, the cor-
rect motivation for growth.

In this chapter, I will first explain the qualities, and in
the next chapter, I will share on "Cultivating Healthy Prophetic Ministries."

This is not a formula that automatically produces growth; this is a lifestyle that we should all implement. When we incorporate this as part of our lifestyle and spiritual DNA, we will see true growth, not only in our gift but also in all areas of our lives.

I want to warn you, we can serve God as members of the Body of Christ, but if we do not have an intimate relationship with Jesus, we will continue living the same life, without fruit or satisfaction. In the first place, everything we do should flow from our intimate relationship with our Heavenly Father. Secondly, we should have a heart that is willing to serve God and others in order to advance the kingdom of God here on earth.

If the reason you are serving is to obtain position or prestige, you've lost the *"revelation of serving."* When we serve with a sincere and genuine heart, this produces advancement in God's Kingdom.

ARE YOU EFFECTIVE IN THE KINGDOM OF GOD?

1 Corinthians 12:4-7: *"Now there are varieties of gifts, but the same Spirit; 5 and there are varieties of service, but the same Lord; and there are varieties of activities, but it is the same God who empowers them all in everyone. To each is given the manifestation of the Spirit for the common good.*

The Holy Spirit is the spring of all gifts, and when we exercise our gifts, we are serving Christ Himself. We all have a different service that we must perform in the kingdom. *"Each one of us is given a spiritual gift so that we help one another."* My first question is, why do you want to exercise your spiritual gift?

The most powerful motivation and reason is to serve the Body of Christ. All ministry should help expand, establish, grow and edify the purposes and plans of God. The primary way we do this is by allowing the Holy Spirit to lead and use us as instruments of transformation.

There are many hearers of the word of God but few do-ers (James 1:22). Many believe in spiritual gifts, but only a few are putting their gifts into practice. This is one of the reasons for which churches cannot impact their communities and there is no growth. They have idle members, which are of no profit for the good of others.

What is your spiritual gift?

What area has God called you to serve?

Many people think that they cannot use their gift in the area of service which God has called them to but the truth is that, they can. For example, people with the gift of prophecy are needed in the children's ministry, so that a prophetic generation will be raised up. Each one of us should learn to use our gifts and also how to impart it to others.

At the same time, ministry can no longer be defined as only within the four walls of the Church. The majority of ministry takes places outside the four walls of the Church, in grocery stores, banks, schools, homes, etc. Your gift is needed outside the four walls of the Church as much as within.

THE GIFT OF PROPHECY IS TO STRENGTHEN THE CHURCH

1 Corinthians 14:3-4: "But he who prophesies speaks edification and exhortation and comfort to men. He who speaks in a tongue edifies himself, but he who prophesies edifies the church."

The Good, Pleasing and Perfect Will of God

In Romans 12:1-8

> I beseech you therefore, brethren, by the mercies of God, that you present your bodies a living sacrifice, holy, acceptable to God, which is your reasonable service. 2 And do not be conformed to this world, but be transformed by the renewing of your mind, that you may prove what is that good and acceptable and perfect will of God. 3 For I say, through the grace given to me, to everyone who is among you, not to think of himself more highly than he ought to think, but to think soberly, as God has dealt to each one a measure of faith. 4 For as we have many members in one body, but all the members do not have the same function, 5 so we, being many, are one body in Christ, and individually members of one another. 6 Having then gifts differing according to the grace that is given to us, let us use them: if prophecy, let us prophesy in proportion to our faith; 7 or ministry, let us use it in our ministering; he who teaches, in teaching; 8 he who exhorts, in exhortation; he who gives, with liberality; he who leads, with diligence; he who shows mercy, with cheerfulness.

In summary, the gifts of the Holy Spirit are to benefit everyone. We must be willing to learn to exercise our spiritual gift in the area we have been called to. We must, for the benefit of the Body of Christ, exercise the gift according to the measure of faith God has given us. This is the good, pleasing, and perfect will of God.

IMPORTANT QUALITIES FOR GROWTH IN THE KINGDOM OF GOD

As children of God, we are called to produce fruits that contribute to the advancement of the Kingdom of God. If you want to grow spiritually, you should serve in the Kingdom. Every person that seeks to grow and mature in their God-given calling must possess certain qualities or attitudes of the heart.

Each one of these qualities requires a heart of service. Many think that while serving, they will not grow spiritually. What they do not know is that God uses service as one of the tools for dealing with obstacles that postpone the spiritual growth in our hearts.

There are many qualities we should have; we are going to focus on a few that are paramount:

Be Faithful

> "and what you have heard from me in the presence of many witnesses entrust to faithful men, who will be able to teach others also." (2 Timothy 2:2; ESV)

I have seen believers who are offended because they were not appointed to be leaders of a team. They do not recognize that they are always late and leave the service early. If you are faithful in the least, you will be entrusted with much says the Lord. Be faithful with your time, service, and do so with excellence. This produces character and stability in your life. A person, who exercises their gift with character, is a person with wisdom.

Be Dedicated

"You know that Stephanas and his household were the first of the harvest of believers in Greece, and they are spending their lives in service to God's people. I urge you, dear brothers and sisters, to submit to them and others like them who serve with such devotion. I am very glad that Stephanas, Fortunatus, and Achaicus have come here. They have been providing the help you weren't here to give me. They have been a wonderful encouragement to me, as they have been to you. You must show your appreciation to all who serve so well." (1 Corinthians 16:15–18; NLT)

Commit yourself to serve and practice your gift in the House of God. Are you willing to spend your time, finances, strengths and abilities to serve the people of God? To be a person of dedication, it takes lots of commitment. You cannot be someone who is dedicated without being committed.

Be Teachable

"'Everyone then who hears these words of mine and does them will be like a wise man who built his house on the rock. And the rain fell, and the floods came, and the winds blew and beat on that house, but it did not fall, because it had been founded on the rock. And everyone who hears these words of mine and does not do them will be like a foolish man who built his house on the sand. And the rain fell, and the floods came, and the winds blew and beat against that house, and it fell, and great was the fall of it.'" (Matthew 7:24–27; ESV)

A person with a teachable spirit is wise; the one who is not teachable is foolish. One reason some believers do not grow in their spiritual lives is because they are not moldable, nor flexible in learning or growth. Do not miss out on learning, even if it is from someone you do not consider capable of teaching you something. Always have a flexible attitude and a teachable heart.

Be Passionate

"This is why I remind you to fan into flames the spiritual gift God gave you when I laid my hands on you. For God has not given us a spirit of fear and timidity, but of power, love, and self-discipline." (2 Timothy 1:6–7; NLT)

"'You are the light of the world—like a city on a hilltop that cannot be hidden. No one lights a lamp and then puts it under a basket. Instead, a lamp is placed on a stand, where it gives light to everyone in the house. In the same way, let your good deeds shine out for all to see, so that everyone will praise your heavenly Father." (Matthew 5:14–16; NLT)

Many people hide and become desperate because they do not see fruit in their lives. God gave you a gift, for you to minister in the body of Christ. If your Pastor or leader asks you to help minister, it is not because they see something bad in your life, it is because they can see the gift God has given you, and to help you develop that gift. If your life is full of fear, it could be that you are not setting the fire for the gift of God ablaze in your life. When one sets the fire ablaze, fear and timidity leave. The power and love of God begin to flow; you start to have self-discipline. Worry when you are not asked to serve. Be passionate about service, and exercising your gift.

Be Watchful

"Follow the pattern of the sound words that you have heard from me, in the faith and love that are in Christ Jesus. By the Holy Spirit who dwells within us, guard the good deposit entrusted to you." (2 Timothy 1:13–14; ESV)

Take care of what has been imparted and taught to you by your spiritual parents and leaders. Take care of the precious truth which they have given you. They paid a very high price for it. Do not take this truth for granted but put it to practice through the power of the Holy Spirit.

Be Responsible

"This charge I entrust to you, Timothy, my child, in accordance with the prophecies previously made about you, that by them you may wage the good warfare, holding faith and a good conscience. By rejecting this, some have made shipwreck of their faith, among whom are Hymenaeus and Alexander, whom I have handed over to Satan that they may learn not to blaspheme." (1 Timothy 1:18–20; ESV)

Be responsible with the prophetic words you receive. Fight the good fight. Maintain a heart clean of all sin. These are our responsibilities that we have. Leaders, mentors and spiritual fathers and mothers impart to us destiny and purpose so we can carry it until it's birthed in our life.

Be Approved

"Do your best to present yourself to God as one approved, a worker who has no need to be ashamed, rightly handling the word of truth. But avoid irreverent babble, for it will lead people into more and more ungodliness, and their talk will spread like gangrene. Among them are Hymenaeus and Philetus," (2 Timothy 2:15–17; ESV)

What do you do to better your life? Do you seek to present yourself before God, and receive His approval? Many receive approval from their parents, but how wonderful it is to realize that God was already speaking His approval to you throughout the week.

Spiritual parents have the responsibility of equipping you for the work that God has for you in His Kingdom, but you have the responsibility of seeking the face of God and being approved by Him.

Lastly, one more important quality that every son and daughter of God must possess is a life of prayer.

A Life of Prayer

"And after he had dismissed the crowds, he went up on the mountain by himself to pray. When evening came, he was there alone," (Matthew 14:23; ESV)

"Then Jesus went with them to a place called Gethsemane, and he said to his disciples, "Sit here, while I go over there and pray."" (Matthew 26:36; ESV)

"And rising very early in the morning, while it was still dark, he departed and went out to a desolate place, and there he prayed." (Mark 1:35; ESV)

"And after he had taken leave of them, he went up on the mountain to pray." (Mark 6:46; ESV)

"In these days he went out to the mountain to pray, and all night he continued in prayer to God." (Luke 6:12; ESV)

"Now it happened that as he was praying alone, the disciples were with him. And he asked them, "Who do the crowds say that I am?"" (Luke 9:18; ESV)

"Now about eight days after these sayings he took with him Peter and John and James and went up on the mountain to pray." (Luke 9:28; ESV)

CHAPTER 9

CULTIVATING HEALTHY PROPHETIC MINISTRIES

"Don't become so well-adjusted to your culture that you fit into it without even thinking. Instead, fix your attention on God. You'll be changed from the inside out. Readily recognize what he wants from you, and quickly respond to it. Unlike the culture around you, always dragging you down to its level of immaturity, God brings the best out of you, develops well-formed maturity in you."

(Romans 12:2, The Message)

With Jesus in mind as the pattern, God had to make Adam and Eve first in His own image and likeness before they could perform their "ministry" in the Garden of Eden. The same is true of us: God wants to make us like Jesus before we can minister fully as Jesus did.

Dr. Bill Hamon

How Can These Things Be?

A healthy prophetic ministry is a by-product of a healthy culture. Culture is not developed over night, but it is prepared and cultivated with a single-hearted pursuit of Heaven's principles and ways. Everything that Jesus did was fueled by Heaven; His perspective was not earthly, but Heavenly. He came to give birth to His Ecclesia that would influence the earthly realm with Heaven. He gave us values, beliefs, and principles that would cultivate Heaven's Culture in our midst.

John 5:19-20 says: *"So Jesus said to them, "Truly, truly, I say to you, the Son can do nothing of his own accord, but only what he sees the Father doing. For whatever the Father does, that the Son does likewise. For the Father loves the Son and shows him all that he himself is doing. And greater works than these will he show him, so that you may marvel."*

The key to releasing Heaven on Earth is found in our relationship with the Father, just as Jesus could do the same. He is our role model and example to follow. After Jesus had left, He expected nothing less of His disciples, and He expects nothing less of us.

"When the Lord Jesus had finished talking with them, he was taken up into heaven and sat down in the place of honor at God's right hand. And the disciples went everywhere and preached, and the Lord worked through them, confirming what they said by many miraculous signs." (Mark 16:19–20; NLT)

How do we cultivate a prophetic culture that is designed after Heaven's Blueprint? What are the keys and principles we can employ to help us establish a long lasting culture that infuses our relationships with life giving power? Let's dive into what a culture is and how we can establish it.

CULTURE | SHAPING THE FUTURE

Culture is defined as *"The sum of attitudes, customs, and beliefs that distinguishes one group of people from another. Culture is transmitted, through language, material objects, ritual, institutions, and art, from one generation to the next.* -The American Heritage® New Dictionary of Cultural Literacy

Culture is the most influential and powerful way to shape the future. Culture is transferable from one generation to another. We can also safely discern an established culture by what values are celebrated. This applies to families, individuals, ministries, and organizations. At the same time, we can see that culture is something people are willing to defend and as we see in some, even die for.

Culture is so powerful, and it can't only influence and shape the lives of a current generation, it's also able to shape the future of generations. Within the Kingdom of God, there is a Biblical Culture that is counter to the common values of the world. We need to be discerning to distinguish between attitudes, traditions, and beliefs that are worldly versus Kingdom Values that promote a healthy culture. How do we do this?

Scripture clearly calls us to be transformed by the renewing of our minds, but it also calls us to guard those things that God has imparted to us.

Romans 12:2 in the Message translations says

> "Don't become so well-adjusted to your culture that you fit into it without even thinking. Instead, fix your attention on God. You'll be changed from the inside out. Readily recognize what he wants from you, and quickly respond to it. Unlike the culture around you, always dragging you down to its level of immaturity, God brings the best out of you, develops well-formed maturity in you."

2 Timothy 1:13-14 declares

> "So keep at your work, this faith and love rooted in Christ, exactly as I set it out for you. It's as sound as the day you first heard it from me. Guard this precious thing placed in your custody by the Holy Spirit who works in us."

PROPHETIC CULTURE | VOICES OF THE NOW AND FUTURE

The prophetic has more power and influence than we can imagine. God created us in His image and likeness; we have God's abilities which when properly activated and employed, can bring Heaven to Earth. We are sons and daughters, agents of Heaven with purpose and power, carriers of His Divine Nature Attributes (DNA) and when you speak, it is Heaven Speaking through you.

We must guard our tongue for this very reason and be careful listeners and slow to speak sometimes. A healthy prophetic voice listens patiently and speaks wisely.

PROPHECY | THE VOICE OF GOD THROUGH US

- Can Reveal God's Purposes and Plans
- It Reveals God's Intimate Voice
- Gives Direction and Protection
- It can instill identity and confidence.

The disciples were taught to pray to the Father by Jesus by asking His Kingdom's Will to be done here on earth. I love how the Living Translation and Easy To Read translation says it:

> "We ask that your kingdom will come now. May your will be done here on earth, just as it is in heaven." (Matthew 6:10; The Living Bible)

The Easy to Read Translation says:

> We pray that your kingdom will come— that what you want will be done here on earth, the same as in heaven.

We are called to proclaim Heaven on Earth. The Holy Spirit showed me in a mental picture the position we all have in Heavenly Places as prophetic voices.

Eyes & Ears in Heaven | Mouth on Earth

If we are to build a prophetic culture that is according to Heaven's blueprint, we must keep our eyes and ears in Heaven and allow our voices to declare what Heaven is like here on Earth.

PRACTICAL WAYS TO CULTIVATE CULTURE

As we learn to cultivate a healthy culture, we can engage in some ways that can help us advance it. To successfully do this, we have to overcome some obstacles, although not impossible, they are the very reason healthy prophetic cultures can't thrive. It will require that we practice a different lifestyle, one of that speaks and celebrates as Heaven does.

GIVE HEAVEN A VOICE

Give a voice to heaven above earth deficiencies and weaknesses. Our experiences either good or bad determine what we give value to. As we voice the value of prophetic ministry, the benefits, and revelation of how to healthily exercise it, we will see more people fear less the prophets and prophetic ministry.

> "And now, dear brothers and sisters, one final thing. Fix your thoughts on what is true, and honorable, and right, and pure, and lovely, and admirable. Think about things that are excellent and worthy of praise." (Philippians 4:8; NLT)

When we value criticism masked as love, we devalue and slow healthy prophetic cultures from thriving. Love corrects by speaking what is true, honorable, right, and pure, lovely, and admirable. Give voice to what empowers, builds and emboldens.

Scripture addresses this very problem that can hurt any ministry from growing.

> "For you have been called to live in freedom, my brothers and sisters. But don't use your freedom to satisfy your sinful nature. Instead, use your freedom to serve one another in love. For the whole law can be summed up in this one command: "Love your neighbor as yourself." But if you are always biting and devouring one another, watch out! Beware of destroying one another." (Galatians 5:13–15; NLT)

CELEBRATE WHAT HEAVEN CELEBRATES

As I shared earlier, you can easily discern the culture many people have by what they celebrate. Sadly, in the Church, making an "example out of people" has been celebrated above Heaven's desire to restore and reconcile. Until we celebrate God's ways of restoration, reconciliation, and relationship, we will hinder the growth of a healthy prophetic culture.

> "Dear brothers and sisters, if another believer is overcome by some sin, you who are godly should gently and humbly help that person back onto the right path. And be careful not to fall into the same temptation yourself. Share each other's burdens, and in this way obey the law of Christ. If you think you are too important to help someone, you are only fooling yourself. You are not that important. Pay careful attention to your own work, for then you will get the satisfaction of a job well done, and you won't need to compare yourself to anyone else. For we are each responsible for our own conduct." (Galatians 6:1–5, NLT)

What are some of the values we need to give a voice to and what are some of the things we need to celebrate to establish a healthy prophetic culture? Let's take a look.

HEALTHY RELATIONSHIPS | RESTORATION & RECONCILIATION

Healthy Prophetic Cultures Produce
- A desire for a healthy relationship and community.
- An atmosphere of possibilities for restoration and reconciliation.
- A deep and profound love for the care of one another.

This is one of the most important values and by-products of a healthy prophetic culture. In Malachi 4:5-6 in the Message Translation, it says:

> "'But also look ahead: I'm sending Elijah the prophet to clear the way for the Big Day of God—the decisive Judgment Day! He will convince parents to look after their children and children to look up to their parents. If they refuse, I'll come and put the land under a curse.'"

Anything less than this is a distortion of God's heart, mind, and will for prophetic ministry. Learn to give relationships a voice that is built upon restoration and reconciliation. Celebrate this important pillar of Heaven's Culture.

PROPHETIC STANDARD
EDIFICATION, EXHORTATION, COMFORT

Another powerful aspect of prophetic ministry and one of the most important ways that we can help cultivate healthy prophetic people is to hold up the standard for personal prophecy.

"But he who prophesies speaks to men for their edification and exhortation and comfort." (1 Corinthians 14:3; MEV)

EDIFICATION | Means to strengthen you to Grow.
EXHORTATION | Means to Embolden You to Believe.
COMFORT | Encourage you to persevere.

Prophetic ministry promotes a culture that builds you up, emboldens you and encourages you. Anything less is a distortion of God's design and culture. This is the standard by which a healthy prophetic community lives and thrives by!

THE FOUNDATION | LOVE

A healthy prophetic culture that has been cultivated through love creates an environment where the pillar of healthy relationships (restoration & reconciliation) and the standard (edification, exhortation, comfort) of the prophetic can be upheld with an empowering grace.

"Most importantly, love each other deeply, because love will cause people to forgive each other for many sins." (1 Peter 4:8; NCV)

COMMON PITFALLS IN A PROPHETIC CULTURE

Like any culture, it has its strengths and weaknesses. A culture based on Heaven is not weak because Heaven lacks, but rather, because of the vessels God uses to transmit it through. God has chosen to release what is perfect through imperfect vessels, and if He is willing to allow it, we must not hinder it, but rather grab ahold of His grace so we may be perfected with every transaction that releases Heaven's Culture here on Earth.

I want to share some common pitfalls you may face as we move into God's prophetic culture as a local community of believers. These pitfalls are not applicable only to a prophetic people, but also to prophets and seasoned prophetic ministers.

UNDERSTANDING PROPHETIC TIMING & MANIFESTATION

Prophets and prophetic ministers can carry a revelation and vision for many years before seeing anyone manifest it. This can create a frustration that sometimes will discourage prophetic ministers from pressing past what seems like a delay.

One example of this is found in the Life of John the Baptist. John himself was the fulfillment of an Old Testament Prophecy found in Isaiah 40:3, he was the *"voice crying out in the wilderness, 'Make straight the way of the Lord.'" John the Baptist baptized* Jesus; he saw the dove descend from Heaven and heard the Voice of the Father confirming Jesus as His Son (John 1). Yet, we see John the Baptist doubt if Jesus was the coming Messiah or if he should wait for another one.

The disciples of John the Baptist came to report to him that the people were amazed at everything Jesus was doing. He had just brought the son of a widow back to life from death. The people were proclaiming and declaring *"God has visited His people!" (Luke 7:11-17)*

> "The disciples of John reported all these things to him. And John, calling two of his disciples to him, sent them to the Lord, saying, "Are you the one who is to come, or shall we look for another?" And when the men had come to him, they said, "John the Baptist has sent us to you, saying, 'Are you the one who is to come, or shall we look for another?'"" (Luke 7:18–20; ESV)

Why did John doubt right after being reported the miracles that Jesus was performing? Prophetic Promises don't always get fulfilled in our timing and certainly not the way we want them to manifest. These are the two reasons John doubted. The latter being one of the most common pitfalls for a prophet. As prophetic ministers, we are not called to make prophetic words manifest the way we envisioned them. Maybe John the Baptist had prepared the way for a Messiah that would establish a physical government with a natural force to rule and reign rather than a spiritual one that would rule and reign through a spiritual body of believers.

Jesus response to John was simply, accept the manifestation of the prophetic promise you prophesied; I like to say, celebrate the fulfillment of the prophetic promise:

> "In that hour he healed many people of diseases and plagues and evil spirits, and on many who were blind he bestowed sight. And he answered them, "Go and tell John what you have seen and heard: the blind receive their sight, the lame walk, lepers are cleansed, and the deaf hear, the dead are raised up, the poor have good news

preached to them. And blessed is the one who is not offended by me.""" (Luke 7:21–23; ESV)

Jesus sends back the messengers with further proofs of His Messiahship and at the same time with a warning to not be offended. Every prophet must go through this test, the season of waiting, diligently prophesying and carrying until the promise is birthed. Don't get offended when suddenly someone begins to walk in the prophetic promise, celebrate it and embrace the fulfillment.

PROPHETICALLY PASTORAL

Prophets and prophetic ministers need to equally develop listening skills as speaking skills to be successful voices of influence. Listening from the heart is the precursor to successful leadership.

Listening communicates:

- I am here.
- I care about you.
- I want to know more about you.

This creates an atmosphere where God's prophetic voice in you can become pastoral, helping establish peace that removes all fears. As prophetic ministers, our goal should not be to just accurately release the Word of the Lord but to also build relationships that can cultivate healthy ways of healing, restoring and reconciling people back into the community.

Prophets and prophetic ministers are filled with vision and destiny, while Pastors are concerned with the present needs of the saints. Being prophetically pastoral means that we can care for the now while casting vision for the destiny and future of the saints. This requires a balancing act, where we are able to direct them towards destiny while not neglecting the present needs they have to get them there in a healthy way.

This brings me to the last pitfall I would like to share with you regarding a prophetic culture. It is one that saints need to understand, and we as leaders must teach and lay a foundation for them to have trust and a healthy relationship with us.

PROPHETIC LEADERSHIP

Understand the role of spiritual authority (pastors, leaders, mentors) as you navigate your prophetic destiny. Leaders by nature have lived life longer than we have, they have if you will, a richer life experience than we do. They are not there to control or dictate your every step; they are there to help you navigate and at times, warn you.

They naturally lead by cultivating and guiding you to community and relationship. Their passion and priority are for you to be led by hearing the Voice of God as a son and daughter of God. Healthy Prophetic Leadership will empower you, but will also hold you accountable.

This is done through relationship, not manipulation or control. The role of leadership is to guide, to role model and demonstrate the paths that lead to success. For this reason, healthy prophetic leadership will lead you to hear God and develop healthy guidelines to keep you aligned to God's heart (grounded and rooted).

CHAPTER 10

THE HOLY SPIRIT

Prophecy—The Voice of the Holy Spirit. The coming of the Holy Spirit, the birth of the Church, and the writing of the Bible did not eliminate the need for the prophetic voice of the Lord; in fact, it intensified that need. Peter insisted that the prophet Joel was speaking of the Church age when he proclaimed, "I will pour out My Spirit in those days, and your sons and daughters shall prophesy" (Acts 2:17).

Dr. Bill Hamon

Prophets and Personal Prophecy

WHO IS THE HOLY SPIRIT?

John 14:15-18 and 26 says "*'If you love me, you will keep my commandments. And I will ask the Father, and he will give you another Helper, to be with you forever, even the Spirit of truth, whom the world cannot receive, because it neither sees him nor knows him. You know him, for he dwells with you and will be in you. "I will not leave you as orphans; I will come to you." (John 14:15–18; ESV)*

"But the Helper, the Holy Spirit, whom the Father will send in my name, he will teach you all things and bring to your remembrance all that I have said to you." (John 14:26; ESV)

Only a person can comfort and be with us—He is the Holy Spirit, the Spirit of Truth. He is not an object or a thing. He is the Spirit of God, which the world cannot receive, understand or see because they do not know Him. We must know the Holy Spirit.

The Apostle John said that the Holy Spirit would dwell and be with us. He will teach us and remind us of everything we should know. How can we ignore Him? He is with us so that we are not orphans.

Our bodies are His temple—many people sin with their body: sexual immorality, drinking alcohol, smoking, getting tattoos, mistreating their body, etc. (1 Corinthians 6:19). They sin because they do not know the Holy Spirit. When they know Him not only as the fire of God but as the Spirit of God, then they will have the fear of God and will be able to overcome all addictions that have set them back. Jesus did not say He would send a fire, an object, an anointing, etc.

He said:

> "And I will ask the Father, and he will give you another Advocate, who will never leave you." The Holy Spirit is one in the same with Jesus Christ and our Heavenly Father. He is not similar or almost like them; He is divine and powerful like Jesus and God the Father.

> "But they rebelled and grieved his Holy Spirit; therefore he turned to be their enemy, and himself fought against them." (Isaiah 63:10; ESV)

Only a person can be grieved if we rebel. How many times have you heard His voice and not obeyed and then we ask, *"Why can't I hear His voice?"*

> "For the Holy Spirit will teach you in that very hour what you ought to say."" (Luke 12:12; ESV)

He will show us and will teach us what we are to say at every moment. He is our divine teacher in the earth. He will give us divine wisdom through Jesus because He speaks what the Father and Jesus speaks.

> "And do not grieve the Holy Spirit of God, by whom you were sealed for the day of redemption." (Ephesians 4:30; ESV)

How often do we grieve Him? To grieve means to sadden. Only someone who loves us can feel this emotion. Only someone that knows us intimately and desperately desires our love can be saddened and anguished by us. Do not ignore the Holy Spirit.

> "Likewise the Spirit helps us in our weakness. For we do not know what to pray for as we ought, but the Spirit himself intercedes for us with groanings too deep for words. And he who searches hearts knows what is the mind of the Spirit, because the Spirit intercedes

for the saints according to the will of God." (Romans 8:26–27; ESV)

The Holy Spirit helps us in our weaknesses. How many times have we done things with our own strength? It says that: He intercedes for us with incredible groaning! He is constantly interceding for us.

"For you did not receive the spirit of slavery to fall back into fear, but you have received the Spirit of adoption as sons, by whom we cry, "Abba! Father!"" (Romans 8:15; ESV)

The Holy Spirit adopted us, and now we can call Him confidently "Abba Father!" He speaks to us of the Father and the Son, and He guides us toward the truth.

If you did not have an earthly father who loved and cared for you; the Holy Spirit is the Spirit of Adoption, and He adopts you today. Do not ignore His presence when He ministers to you because He offers security, love and sets you free from all rejection.

"Nevertheless, I tell you the truth: it is to your advantage that I go away, for if I do not go away, the Helper will not come to you. But if I go, I will send him to you. And when he comes, he will convict the world concerning sin and righteousness and judgment: concerning sin, because they do not believe in me; concerning righteousness, because I go to the Father, and you will see me no longer; concerning judgment, because the ruler of this world is judged. "I still have many things to say to you, but you cannot bear them now. When the Spirit of truth comes, he will guide you into all the truth, for he will not speak on his own authority, but whatever he hears he will speak, and he will declare to you the things that are to come. He will glorify me, for he will take what is mine and declare it to you. All that the Father has is mine; therefore I said that he will take what is mine and declare it to you." (John 16:7–15; ESV)

The New Living Translation reads:

"But in fact, it is best for you that I go away, because if I don't, the Advocate won't come. If I do go away, then I will send him to you. 8 And when he comes, he will convict the world of its sin, and of God's righteousness, and of the coming judgment. 9 The world's sin is that it refuses to believe in me. 10 Righteousness is available because I go to the Father, and you will see me no more. 11 Judgment will come because the ruler of this world has already been judged. 12 "There is so much more I want to tell you, but you can't bear it now. 13 When the Spirit of truth comes, he will guide you into all truth. He will not speak on his own but will tell you what he has heard. He will tell you about the future. 14 He will bring me glory by telling you whatever he receives from me. 15 All that belongs to the Father is mine; this is why I said, 'The Spirit will tell you whatever he receives from me.'

WITNESS VS. EVIDENCE

"For there are three that testify: the Spirit and the water and the blood; and these three agree." (1 John 5:7–8; ESV)

For someone to be a witness, they must be able to explain, speak of, have seen, or experienced something to be able to give testimony. Everything else is evidence. The fire, anointing, power, gifts, and fruits are all evidence of the Holy Spirit, but He is a Witness! You may be able to see the evidence but the question is, are you a witness? Acts 1 says that the Holy Spirit would come upon us so we may be witnesses.

You cannot be a witness if you have only seen others experience the manifestations of the Holy Spirit. They might not be witnesses of the Holy Spirit but only of His power and presence.

We must be witnesses of the Holy Spirit, not only of His presence. How often do you speak with the Holy Spirit?

How much time do you spend with Him? The reason believers struggle with sin is they do not have a relationship with the Holy Spirit, and they do not fear offending, saddening, or turning the Holy Spirit away from their lives.

> "And we are witnesses to these things, and so is the Holy Spirit, whom God has given to those who obey him."" (Acts 5:32; ESV)

The Holy Spirit is our witness of the powerful Savior and Redeemer; Jesus Christ. Do you know Him? Or do you only know of Jesus Christ simply because others speak of Him? Many believers have knowledge of the Holy Spirit, but very few have a relationship with Him.

A believer who has an intimate relationship with the Holy Spirit is filled with His presence. The Book of Acts teaches us that we are to have a relationship with the Holy Spirit and continuously be filled with His presence.

The Apostles and believers of the early church would not do anything without the direction of the Holy Spirit. They multiplied because the Spirit of God was among them. When they prayed, the earth would shake, and they would boldly speak the word of God. When they would confront the powers of the occult, it was through the Holy Spirit. There were miracles, signs, wonders, deliverance, and multiplication all because they were witnesses of the Holy Spirit.

> Acts 4:8— Then Peter, filled with the Holy Spirit, said to them: "Rulers and elders of the people!

> Acts 4:31— After they prayed, the place where they were meeting was shaken. And they were all filled with the Holy Spirit and spoke the word of God boldly.

Acts 6:5— This proposal pleased the whole group. They chose Stephen, a man full of faith and of the Holy Spirit; also Philip, Procorus, Nicanor, Timon, Parmenas, and Nicolas from Antioch, a convert to Judaism.

Acts 11:24— He was a good man, full of the Holy Spirit and faith, and a great number of people were brought to the Lord.

Acts 13:8-11— But Elymas the sorcerer (for that is what his name means) opposed them and tried to turn the proconsul from the faith. 9 Then Saul, who was also called Paul, filled with the Holy Spirit, looked straight at Elymas and said, 10 "You are a child of the devil and an enemy of everything that is right! You are full of all kinds of deceit and trickery. Will you never stop perverting the right ways of the Lord? 11 Now the hand of the Lord is against you. You are going to be blind for a time, not even able to see the light of the sun." Immediately mist and darkness came over him, and he groped about, seeking someone to lead him by the hand.

Acts 13:52— And the disciples were filled with joy and with the Holy Spirit.

WHAT DOES THE HOLY SPIRIT DO?

As I mentioned before, He does only what a person would do. An object does not speak, convince, and is not saddened. Review the following Scriptures and get to know Him.

- He convicts the world: When he comes, he will prove the world to be in the wrong about sin and righteous-ness and judgment (John16:8)
- He teaches: He will teach you all things (John 14:26; See also Neh. 9:20; John 16:13-15; 1 John 2:27)

- The Spirit speak: Because you are his sons, God sent the Spirit of his Son into our hearts, the Spirit who calls out, "Abba,[a] Father." (Gal. 4:6)
- The Spirit intercedes: But the Spirit himself intercedes for us through wordless groans. (Ro. 8:26)
- The Spirit Guides: Led by the Spirit (Gal 5:18; cf. Acts 8:29; 10:19; 13:2; 16:6-7; 20:23; Ro. 8:14)
- The Spirit appoints man to a specific work: the Holy Spirit said, "Set apart for me Barnabas and Saul for the work to which I have called them." (Acts 13:2; cf. Acts 20:28)
- The Spirit Himself is submitted to a plan: (John 15:26)
- The Spirit ministers, He regenerates (John 3:6), He seals (Eph. 4:30), He baptizes (1 Cor. 12:13), He fills (Eph 5:18)
- Man can make the Spirit angry (Isa. 63:10), Sadden Him (Eph. 4:30), Resist Him (1 Thess. 5:19), Blaspheme against Him (Matt. 12:31), Lie to Him (Acts 5:3), Give affront (Acts 10:29), and can Speak against Him (Matt. 12:32)

SHOULD YOU RECEIVE
THE HOLY SPIRIT?

John 20:22— And with that he breathed on them and said, "Receive the Holy Spirit.

How can we receive the Holy Spirit? There is a difference between receiving and developing a relationship with the Holy Spirit. Receiving Him requires nothing more than hunger, a desperate desire and faith that He is our counselor.

In 2005, I received the Holy Spirit; I was filled with His love, joy, and peace. I remember my greatest desire was to hear His voice. I wanted nothing else but to hear His voice. I did not want a gift or anointing. I only desired to hear His voice. The insatiable hunger for His voice, and presence took me to a supernatural experience with Him.

I was attending one of Pastor Benny Hinn's Youth Conferences. My friend and I had been fasting, to receive the Holy Spirit's infilling. In the middle of the preaching, my friend was filled with the Holy Spirit, but I did not, and for a moment, I was worried, thinking I would not be filled, I would not receive the Spirit. We were in a separate area because the main conference room was full and they sent us into another room.

We were with the church's youth group. For a moment, we all went to a corner to pray, and one by one, they were filled with the Holy Spirit, but I still had not received anything.

I had for more than one year desired to be filled. In our church, they did not teach about being filled with the Holy Spirit. They would speak of Him, but we were not witnesses of Him. I had studied the Gospels, and the Book of Acts; I knew that the Holy Spirit is a promise from our Heavenly Father.

I remember reading Acts 2:16-18:

> "No, this is what was spoken by the prophet Joel: 'In the last days, God says, I will pour out my Spirit on all people. Your sons and daughters will prophesy, your young men will see visions, your old men will dream dreams. Even on my servants, both men and women, I will pour out my Spirit in those days, and they will prophesy.'"

This promise sustained me for a year, as I cried out and desired His Holy Spirit. When the event was coming to an end, I thought "If it does not happen today, it will be the next time," but I did not know I was about to receive a surprise that would transform my life forever.

I would meditate on God's word and the promise that the Holy Spirit is for me and all believers. I asked myself, "How will I know if I received the Holy Spirit and not something else?" This is a question many people have and is also one of the reasons they do not receive the Holy Spirit because of the fear of receiving something that is not of God, but the Word of God has an answer:

> Luke 11:9-13, "So I say to you: Ask and it will be given to you; seek and you will find; knock and the door will be opened to you. 10 For everyone who asks receives; the one who seeks finds; and to the one who knocks, the door will be opened.11 "Which of you fathers, if your son asks for[a] a fish, will give him a snake instead? 12 Or if he asks for an egg, will give him a scorpion? 13 If you then, though you are evil, know how to give good gifts to your children, how much more will your Father in heaven give the Holy Spirit to those who ask him!"

When the conference was almost over, we were able to enter the main room because many people were starting to leave. When we walked in, Pastor Benny Hinn said, "Ask for what you want, and He will give it to you in this moment." And I said, "Lord, I want to be filled with your Holy Spirit." At that very moment, I started to speak in tongues. It was something supernatural and powerful. I immediately started hearing His voice. And He told me "Look to your left." I saw a child praying, and the Holy Spirit said to me: "Tell him to receive what he is asking for." I kneeled down and told the child, "Receive what you are asking for." In that moment, the little boy fell to the ground, shaking under the power of the Holy Spirit.

From that day on, I've desired to hear His sweet voice. I desire to know Him more, hearing Him, and seeing Him more than anything else. Receive Him now, open your heart; He is ready to enter and fill your heart with His presence, love, and joy. But more than anything, He is longing for you to know Him.

To be able to develop a relationship with Him, you must be persistent. The Apostle in Acts chapter 1 received a command-ment from Jesus "vs. 4-5. On one occasion, while he was eating with them, he gave them this command: "Do not leave Jerusalem, but wait for the gift my Father promised, which you have heard me speak about. For John baptized with[a] water, but in a few days you will be baptized with[b] the Holy Spirit."

Wait until our Father sends you the gift He promised. There is a price to pay for being witnesses of His power and presence. It is not about a few minutes of prayer; it is only those who pay the price of prayer, and intimacy with the Holy Spirit that can truly be witnesses.

I do not only desire to speak of Him; I want to be His witness!

Activation

- Repent for ignoring Him. Tell Him that you not only want to know of His presence, and power, but that you want to speak with Him, you want to hear His voice and see His presence.

- Long for Him, be hungry for His voice and presence. Commit to being persistent until you obtain an intimate relationship with Him.
- Receive being filled with the Holy Spirit; activate the gift of speaking in tongues.
- Obey His voice when He speaks to you; do not be afraid of taking a risk. He backs His word.

In a piece of paper write down *"The Holy Spirit says: Son or Daughter" by faith begin to write what the Holy Spirit shows you.....*

Q & A

There are many questions about the prophetic and prophecy. At the core of these questions is a desire to hear God and understand what He is asking of us. In this section, I want to share with you some insight and help bring clarity to some of those questions. The answers I provide are not meant to be the final answer; I'm sharing from the Scripture and personal experience. My hope is to provide adequate clarification regarding some of the questions that you may seek God for and the answers you need from Him.

HOW DOES GOD'S VOICE SOUND LIKE?

WE WERE DESIGNED TO HEAR HIS VOICE

The question is frequently asked because we have a belief that God is going to make it difficult and hard for us to hear Him. As if, we may need to decode His voice or understand some cryptic message. There is no doubt, that when you hear the voice of God, it is powerful and full of majesty as King David described it in Psalms 29:4. Jesus said: *"'My sheep hear my voice, and I know them, and they follow me" (John 10:27).* It is in our DNA, our design, the ability, perception, and discernment to hear and follow Him. It only takes learning some of the ways that God speaks, finding it and embracing it.

When I particularly hear the Voice of God, it comes through a thought. I remember the day I heard one of our Apostolic Prophetic Trainers say, "God's voice often sounds like your thoughts!" Something clicked, a light bulb turned on in my head! I realized that I could fine-tune my heart and spiritual ears to hear God better. At that moment, I began to embrace that the primary way God speaks to me is through my thoughts. Many times, it feels like a thought that was dropped in my mind unexpectedly.

Another aspect of hearing God is that He may not speak through sound, like an audible voice, but at times God speaks to us through dreams, visions, experiences, and via our natural senses. I say this, to encourage you, not to limit yourself to only hearing a voice. There are times when God will speak to you or reveal to you something through your emotions or physical body.

There are many times when I can sense sadness over an individual, their outward appearance may seem joyful or content, but in my emotions, I felt sadness. I've learned to trust God, to believe He is faithful. This does not mean we should come to a person and boldly declare "The Lord says, you are depressed!" Maybe, God is sharing with us the reality of their emotions so that we can speak a word of encouragement.

I mentioned that God might speak to us through our physical body, this happens to me frequently when I operate in Word of Knowledge. I sometimes may feel pain or touch in a specific area of my body, revealing an area that God wants to touch in the physical body of the person. I heard Randy Clark one time say, he always checks his body before going to minister healing, to make sure he is aware of his physical body. So that when he begins to minister, he does not attribute a pain or discomfort to a word of knowledge when in reality he had something prior to ministering. Very wise.

God speaks, that is settled, how He sounds or how He speaks to you, is a process of discovery. Do you see pictures? Do you have a lot of dreams? Do you sense things in your emotions? Do you frequently have thoughts drop into your mind that you were not expecting about someone? Ask God for clarity and begin to discover how He speaks to you.

CAN GOD'S VOICE SOUND LIKE SOME OTHER PERSON?

When the young Prophet Samuel was being trained to hear the voice of God at the Temple. Scripture says

> "'Then the Lord called Samuel, and he said, "Here I am!" and ran to Eli and said, "Here I am, for you called me." But he said, "I did not call; lie down again." So he went and lay down. And the Lord called again, "Samuel!" and Samuel arose and went to Eli and said, "Here I am, for you called me." But he said, "I did not call, my son; lie down again." Now Samuel did not yet know the Lord, and the word of the Lord had not yet been revealed to him. And the Lord called Samuel again the third time. And he arose and went to Eli and said, "Here I am, for you called me." Then Eli perceived that the Lord was calling the boy. Therefore Eli said to Samuel, "Go, lie down, and if he calls you, you shall say, 'Speak, Lord, for your servant hears.' " So Samuel went and lay down in his place." (1 Samuel 3:4–9; ESV)

Samuel was hearing the voice of God, but it sounded to him like the voice of Eli. It was not until Eli perceived that God was speaking to Samuel that he was able to give young Samuel wisdom and instructions that led him to recognize how God was speaking to him. I use this example to share with you that God can sound like others, in this case, God was using a voice that was familiar to Samuel to train Him to hear. I remember, one time, God spoke to me through a prophet in my dream. I was going through a difficult season and one night, I had a dream, and this prophet began to just speak encouragement to me.

In the dream, I knew it was God speaking through Him. He was using someone whom I admire and I'm familiar with to encourage me. At that time, I was crying out to God desperately to speak to me, but most likely, the burden of what I was going through could not let me hear God for myself. So He had to speak to me through someone else.

CAN I AT ANY TIME HEAR FROM GOD?

Yes and the answer to this question challenges the very fiber of our theology and revelation of God. How can God speak to anyone at any time? The reality is, many believers already have faith to hear God through Scripture. Frequently, they dedicate time with the intention and purpose to hear God as they study His word (Romans 8:17). If we believe that God can speak to us through Scripture, it should not be a stretch to believe that God can speak to us through His Holy Spirit.

Faith is the key to hearing the Voice of God at any time and any place. Faith simply means trusting in His faithfulness. Jesus said that His sheep would hear His voice and follow Him (John 10:17). The Apostle Paul declared that those who are led by the voice of God's Holy Spirit are sons of God (Romans 8:14). If you are born-again, you can hear Him and be led by Him at anytime and anywhere. Only engage in trust and faith that as a Good Father; He wants to have a relationship with you and lead you to your destiny.

DID GOD STOP SPEAKING NOW THAT WE HAVE THE BIBLE?

No, God did not stop speaking now that we have the Bible. What God has stopped doing is writing scriptures through prophets and apostles. His word is inerrant, and no prophet or minister can add or take away from it. The primary job of any minister or prophet is not to add new revelation or doctrines but to help illuminate, reveal, and activate the word of God to equip the saints for the work of the Ministry.

His voice is still actively speaking guiding and leading us into all truth.

> "But when he—the Spirit of truth—comes, he will guide you into all the truth. For he will not speak from himself, but whatever he hears he will speak, and he will proclaim to you the things to come." (John 16:13; LEB)

DOES HE YELL OR DOES HE WHISPER?

In 1 Kings 19, Elijah had just confronted the prophets of Baal at Mount Carmel. After Elijah had confronted them and demonstrated that God was the true God, he defeated all the false prophets. Jezebel found out what Elijah had done and sent a messenger to him saying:

> "Then Jezebel sent a messenger to Elijah, saying, 'Thus may the gods do to me, and may they add to it, surely at this time tomorrow I will make your life as the life of one of them!' Then he became afraid, got up, and fled for his life. He came to Beersheba which belongs to Judah, and he left his servant there." (1 Kings 19:2–3; LEB)

Elijah was afraid and therefore ran for his life and hid in a cave. While he was in the cave, the Word of the Lord came to him asking why he was hiding in a cave? God led Elijah to stand on the mountain so He could speak to Him. It was at this moment that God revealed Himself to Elijah in a unique way:

> "And he said, 'Go out and stand on the mount before the Lord.' And behold, the Lord passed by, and a great and strong wind tore the mountains and broke in pieces the rocks before the Lord, but the Lord was not in the wind. And after the wind an earthquake, but the Lord was not in the earthquake. And after the earthquake a fire, but the Lord was not in the fire. And after the fire the sound of a low whisper. And when Elijah heard it, he wrapped his face in his cloak and went out and stood at the entrance of the cave. And behold, there came a voice to him and said, 'What are you doing here, Elijah?' He said, 'I have been very jealous for the Lord, the

God of hosts. For the people of Israel have forsaken your covenant, thrown down your altars, and killed your prophets with the sword, and I, even I only, am left, and they seek my life, to take it away.' And the Lord said to him, 'Go, return on your way to the wilderness of Damascus. And when you arrive, you shall anoint Hazael to be king over Syria.'" (1 Kings 19:11–15; ESV)

A strong windstorm, earthquake, and fire manifested, but God chose not to reveal His voice through those natural events, He decided to use a whisper. I believe that God will speak to each one of us in such a way that we can hear Him. Elijah was already afraid, and maybe God could have chosen to speak through the windstorm, earthquake, and fire to show Elijah how powerful He was and not to be scared. He chose a whisper, which I believe speaks to God's comfort and peace that Elijah needed at that very moment to gain courage again. I don't believe God yells. The truth is that any experience of hearing God is supernatural and with it carries an intensity that will affect us. But I believe God chooses that which can transform us and impacts us so we can hear Him and have a relationship with Him.

CAN GOD USE SECULAR MOVIE TO SPEAK TO ME?

I have heard many people comment that a certain movie touched their heart and felt as if God was speaking to them through it. I believe God can speak to us in many ways. I would like to warn, although God may speak to you, we cannot use movies to base our theology or doctrine. Also, we must filter everything we hear through His word and character. What we hear spiritually must line up with

God's Kingdom purpose and will, His character, word, and principles.

HOW DO I KNOW WHAT GOD IS SAYING IS FROM HIM?

There is one primary way for us to make sure we know what God is saying is from Him. His word reveals to us His purposes, plans, character, values, and principles. Anything that we hear must align with His word. God will not ask us anything that will violate His Character and Kingdom. It's important that everyone have regular Bible study so that you can fill yourself with the Word of God.

Secondly, I highly recommend that anyone that is learning to hear God should submit themselves to spiritual authority before making any major decisions. They will be able to help you with wisdom, with even a different perspective that can help you best make a decision according to the will of God. Where many people miss God is not in hearing Him but in the process of application of personal prophecy. Here are some practical things to do:

- *Write it down – Make sure you write it down so you can* easily read it and access it at any time.
- *Search Scriptures – That back up what* was prophesied over you or what you heard. For example, if you heard from God that you are going to be used to heal the sick, begin to study about healing. Or if God said you would travel to the nations, begin to search God scriptures for His heart about the nations. If God said you would be a business person, begin to understand and search for God's

principles on economy, stewardship, and administration. Scripture has these.

- *Share it with your Pastor, Mentor or Leader* – set up a time to share with them what God spoke to you. Ask them for wisdom and pray with them about the decisions you need to make.

WHY DOES SOMEONE STOP HEARING THE VOICE OF GOD?

God is always trying to speak to us; He goes through great lengths to reach out to us. I don't believe someone can stop hearing unless they willingly refuse to obey His voice or lack the faith (ignorance) to believe they can hear His voice. I do believe it can become difficult and at the same time cause you to miss your blessing. Yet, God is merciful and graceful, if the Scripture says that *"while we were still sinners He died for us"* (Romans 5:6-8), I don't think even sin would stop Him from speaking, it is dependent on our faith and obedience to hear Him.

> "For he is our God, and we are the people of his pasture, and the sheep of his hand. Today, if you hear his voice, do not harden your hearts, as at Meribah, as on the day at Massah in the wilderness, when your fathers put me to the test and put me to the proof, though they had seen my work. For forty years I loathed that generation and said, 'They are a people who go astray in their heart, and they have not known my ways.' Therefore I swore in my wrath, 'They shall not enter my rest.'" (Psalm 95:7–11; ESV)

WHAT CAN BLOCK US FROM HEARING HIS VOICE CLEARLY/MAKING IT FOGGY?

There are two primary ways that hearing God's voice can become difficult, blocked or foggy. One of them is sin, when someone has been living a lifestyle of sin, they become insensitive to God's voice and ways. The second way is lack of faith, which is a result of lack of knowledge. Sensitivity to God's voice comes through intimacy and revelational knowledge, which is void of sin and disobedience.

It's important we keep our hearts pure, our minds holy and continually exercise our spiritual ears and eyes so we can hear God. Allow the Word of God to penetrate your heart and cleanse you, purify you, and make you sensitive to His voice.

> "For the word of God is living and active, sharper than any two-edged sword, piercing to the division of soul and of spirit, of joints and of marrow, and discerning the thoughts and intentions of the heart. And no creature is hidden from his sight, but all are naked and exposed to the eyes of him to whom we must give account." (Hebrews 4:12–13; ESV)

> "But solid food is for the mature, for those who have their powers of discernment trained by constant practice to distinguish good from evil." (Hebrews 5:14; ESV)

ABOUT THE AUTHOR

E dgar for over 10 years has be a part of Christian International Ministries Network founded by Bishop Bill Hamon the Father of the Prophetic Movement. His training and upbringing has come through personal mentoring under the House of the Prophets. He is part of the ministry staff, an instructor in the Apostolic Prophetic Trainings (APT) and Vision Leadership Institute. Under the leading of the Holy Spirit, he flows under a Prophetic-Apostolic Teaching mantle that brings reformation to the lives of believers and transforming their hearts to be passionate seekers of God's will and purpose for their life.

He along with his wife, Victoria, are coordinators of Christian International en Español, they are Associate Ordained Ministers of Vision Church @ Christian International under Apostles Tom and Jane Hamon. They travel nationally and internationally reaching souls, families and nations for Christ. In May of 2016 they joined the Pastoral Team of Vision Church Fort Walton Beach under Pastor's Ned and Laci Maraman. Edgar and Victoria currently reside in Santa Rosa Beach, Fl with their sons, Josiah and David.

www.ingramcontent.com/pod-product-compliance
Lightning Source LLC
Chambersburg PA
CBHW051834040426

42447CB00006B/515